THE
SHEFFIELD
BOOK
OF
DAYS

MARGARET DRINKALL

First published 2012

The History Press
The Mill, Brimscombe Port
Stroud, Gloucestershire, GL5 2QG
www.thehistorypress.co.uk

British Library Cataloguing in Publication Data.
A catalogue record for this book is available from the British
Library.

ISBN 978 0 7524 6470 1

Typesetting and origination by The History Press
Printed in India
Manufacturing managed by Jellyfish Print Solutions Ltd

JANUARY 1ST

1880: Entitled 'A New Years Eve in Sheffield', an account of the previous night's activities was published in the *Sheffield Independent*. The report read: 'In consequence of the inclemency of the weather, the streets were less busy last night than is customary. There was in fact almost an entire absence of pedestrians until midnight, when the public and beer houses – which had an hours grace – got rid of their customers. But the streets even then were soon at peace broken only by the "waits" who, with an eye to coppers, sang their ditties in spite of the wind and rain. The old year took its departure amid an appropriate accompaniment of rain for tears. A "watch night" service was celebrated in most of the Wesleyan Chapels'. In contrast to the informal entertainment, the service at the parish church, which started at 11 p.m. held a large congregation. Revd A.J. Tweedie read the parable of the Ten Virgins and at 11.55 p.m., he urged them to have five minutes of silent prayer. He then announced that 'now that the old year of 1879 has passed away we have commenced a new year in the journey of our life'. The service then closed with a hymn. (*Sheffield Independent*)

JANUARY 2ND

1613: One of the earliest surveys ever recorded was undertaken, which indicated the poverty of the people of the town at that time. The survey or early census was undertaken by the Ecclesiastical authorities to assess the numbers of ratepayers able to pay tithes to the Church. It reads: 'Survaie [*sic*] of the towns of Sheffield by twenty-four of the most sufficient inhabitants in the towne. There are 2,207 people of which 725 are not able to live without the charity of their neighbours being all begging poore [*sic*]. There are 100 households which relieve others but are poor artificers not one of which can keep a team on his own lande [*sic*] and not above ten who have grounds of their own on which to keep a cow. 160 householders are not able to relieve others such though they beg not. Many of them are not able to abide the storme [*sic*] of one fortnight sickness but would be thereby driven to beggary. There are 1,222 children and servants of the said householders the greatest part of which such as live off small wages and are constrained to work to provide them with the necessities.' (Leader, R., *Sheffield Local Directory*, Sheffield Independent Press, 1830)

JANUARY 3RD

1830: The state of public footpaths in Sheffield was criticized in the *Sheffield Independent*, with the report stating: 'After the required cleansing had been performed, it sometimes happened that a sudden fall of snow or the industry of schoolboys created a nice slide within a foot of one's doorway. A shovelful of "slack" (coal dust) immediately put on such hazardous areas could have saved a sprain or a broken limb. Many of the accidents which occur in Sheffield at the moment could be prevented. On Wednesday, Mr Simmons, a traveller from Birmingham, was getting out of his gig to make a call when he stepped onto the ice and fell, breaking the cap of his knee. On the evening of the same day, a respectable female fell in Coalpit Lane and dislocated her shoulder. On Sunday evening Mr Wood, a dyer of the Wicker, slipped down and fractured a leg. On the same day Mr John Gardner of Pea Croft fell and broke his arm. The vigilance of the Police Inspectors does much to keep such accidents to a minimum, but if more householders would do the same the streets of the city might be in a fitter state for perambulation that they are at present'. (*Sheffield Independent*)

JANUARY 4TH

1879: It was reported today in the *Sheffield Post* that the Princess of Wales donated £50 towards the relief of the poor in Sheffield. The donation, accompanied by a letter, expressed her regret to which Her Royal Highness has heard of the prevailing industrial distress in the town. It was also reported that the Duke of Norfolk (Lord of the manor of Sheffield) had subscribed £500 to the fund and the Duchess of Norfolk £100. The Home Secretary has written to the Mayor for information as to the extent of the industrial distress and the local means of dealing with it. Among the sums received by the Mayor of Sheffield was one of £25 donated by Florence Nightingale, who attached a letter stating that: 'If I might breathe a hope as earnest as that Sheffield will be tided ever these sad, sad times, it would be that her men might learn from them a lesson of prudence and manly self control and that when good times come again, as pray God they may, they will use their higher wages so as to become capital instead of waste.'

The reporter also noted that: 'In Sheffield at present the distress is increasing and the total cost of subscriptions now amount to over £7,000'. (*Sheffield Post*)

JANUARY 5TH

1864: On this day, the newspapers reported Margaret Godfrey's escape from the women's prison at the Town Hall. A police officer was scrubbing the parade room floor and had cause to go into the women's yard for water. Missing Godfrey, he was told that she was in the water closet. When he returned once more, he called out to her and received no reply. The walls of the prison yard are topped with iron spikes and are 20ft high. It was felt that to escape this way dressed in petticoats would be impossible, but when officers examined the wall they found marks of her escape. On reaching the top of the wall, Godfrey would have thrown herself 16 to 17ft down to the ground as there was nothing in the wall to help her descent. The chief constable, on being told of the escape, ordered some men to go to the Sheffield Infirmary to make enquires. There she was found being treated for injury to her spine. She had arrived there in a cab driven by a man of her acquaintance and it is thought that he had helped her to make her escape. (*Sheffield Independent*)

JANUARY 6TH

1900: Today saw a celebration for Mr Edwin Waters, the master of Sheffield Fir Vale workhouse, who had just celebrated his silver wedding. He had been master of the workhouse for seventeen years, and the guardians took the opportunity to present him with a gift of a cutlery set as a token of their respect for the 'man who had served at his post through the many changes which have been seen in Poor Law administration'. He and his wife also received gifts and presents from the other officers of the workhouse. Mr Waters entertained the members of the board along with friends at his home. Making the presentation, Alderman Wycliffe Wilson told him that 'he had always worked to improve the administration of the house, and that under his direction his discipline was highly beneficial to those placed in his care'. Another guardian, one Mr Hoyland, spoke about the ready cheerfulness of both the master and matron of the workhouse. Mr Waters thanked the guardians for their gifts and their generous comments. He said that 'he was pleased to hear that his work had exercised a good influence at the workhouse'. (*Yorkshire Post*)

January 7th

1857: An incident occurred on this day which arguably proves the old saying 'there is no fool like an old fool'. A retired gentleman of the town sauntered into the marketplace, where he was accosted by a stranger dressed in the garb of a horse dealer. This man told him that he had come to buy a pony for his son but had no idea where to find the owner. Strangely, just at that moment, the seller of the pony appeared. The horse dealer made him an offer for the pony, but the owner, affecting to be insulted by some rude observation, refused the deal. The dealer then proposed that the old gentleman buy the pony for him and the old gentleman and the seller then went to an adjoining public house, where negotiations were sealed and the old man was induced to hand over £4 to seal the bargain. He left the public house to inform his 'friend' of the successful negotiations, only to find that he had mysteriously disappeared. He returned back to the public house to find the seller had also decamped with his money. The poor old man returned home wiser for the lesson. (*Sheffield Times*)

JANUARY 8TH

1889: Newspapers today printed an account of a traction engine accident, which had overturned at Carbrook the previous Saturday. The incident took place on Weedon Street close to the Congregational Chapel. An open brook runs down the north side of the street, and, in some places, the bank was broken and as a result the road was extremely narrow and dangerous. The traction engine and two attached wagons were turning out of Carbrook into Weedon Street when the driver's vision was impaired by fog. Inevitably the traction engine turned over into the brook. The flywheel and some of the gearing was broken off and one of the wagons had been dragged in after it. Fortunately, of the three men involved, only slight injuries were sustained. Men were at work all day Sunday digging down the embankment, making a course in which to drag the fallen machine out of the brook. Another traction engine was brought to drag it to an upright position and held it there by the means of a wire rope. Yet another engine was brought in to pull it out of the brook. By Sunday evening the mission was accomplished and the area was cleared. (*Sheffield Telegraph*)

JANUARY 9TH

1831: An inquest was held on the body of a newborn baby who had been found dead in a pit at Ballifield, near Handsworth. The pit was 52 yards deep and the surgeon, Mr Nicholson, estimated that the child had been dead for around a week. He told the jury and coroner Mr Badger that the child, which was full term, had a fractured lower jaw, contusions on the head, and the bone of the head was more than ordinarily separated. He gave his opinion that the contusions and the skull fracture had caused the death of the baby. Although he could not estimate whether or not the child had breathed upon being born, he believed that the baby may have been born dead. George Fowler, a collier who found the body on January 8th at 9.30 a.m., described how the corpse had no covering on it. Another witness, Susannah Wilkinson, gave evidence of another girl who it was suspected had recently given birth under mysterious circumstances. Several other witnesses were questioned about the identification of the suspected mother of the child. Their testimony justified an examination of her person by the surgeon, who reported to the jury that she had not been delivered of a child. (*The Standard*)

January 10th

1821: On this day a murder was reported in the *Sheffield Independent*. Its readers were told that: 'On Thursday night, a woman named Sarah Crowder residing in Red Croft was found dead in her bed. She had been seen by several of her neighbours in the course of the afternoon and had not made any particular complaint of illness. But it is generally supposed that the poor creature had fallen prey to want, as she could not procure even the common necessities of life. Crowder had scarcely a garment left to shelter her from inclemency of the weather. At the inquest the coroner was informed that she had for some time being separated from her husband, who had deserted her and her two children to cohabit with another woman in the town. She had only 4s a week allowed to her from her husband to support herself and the children. In order to eke out this miserable pittance, Crowder had been compelled to part with nearly every article of apparel and even the covering from the bed.' The reporter stated that 'a more heart-rending scene of nakedness and starvation than that which this poor woman and her children exhibited was never witnessed'. (*Sheffield Independent*)

JANUARY 11TH

1873: A serious riot took place in Sheffield. In *A History of Sheffield*, David Hey stated that 'it has become a matter of common occurrence in the town to hear of street rows. It would appear that in some areas, the roughs are able to carry everything their own way in spite of law, magistrates and police'. At around 11.30 p.m., two police constables who were on duty in the town, noted some 'roughs' jostling passers-by, annoying both them and the tradesmen. They were asked to stop but instead they started to pelt the constables with sticks, refuse and stones. Despite this, the constables managed to capture one of the gang and took him to a house on Hoyle Street for his own protection. A mob of about 100 people grouped together and began smashing the windows of the house and throwing stones at the doors, which left the occupiers terrified. The two constables had no option but to release the prisoner and attempt to get out of the house unharmed. They managed to return to the police station, where reinforcements were quickly sent to the scene and, before any more damage could be inflicted, the crowd was dispersed. (Hey, D., *A History of Sheffield,* Carnegie Publishing, 1998)

JANUARY 12TH

1866: On this day, a woman lay in the Infirmary recovering from the poisonous effects of arsenic she had taken in an attempt to kill herself. The young woman (18) called Ellen Dalton lived with her mother on Steel Bank and had worked for the last three years at Messrs Brookes on Carlisle Street. The previous morning she had left the house to go to work after having words with her mother. At lunch time she began vomiting copiously and almost became insensible. A surgeon, Mr Arden, was called and he asked both her and her friends what she had eaten but did not get a sensible answer from anyone concerned. The girl was sent home and after Mr Arden visited her again this morning she told him what she had done. It seems that nine months ago she was being pestered by a man she did not want and had bought, at different times, four-penny worth of arsenic with which to kill herself. After the row with her mother at about 11.30 a.m., she had taken a teaspoon of arsenic in some water. The surgeon told her that because she had taken so much; her body had ejected the poison, thereby saving her life. (*Sheffield Independent*)

JANUARY 13TH

1873: It was reported that the authorities of the Manchester, Sheffield and Lincolnshire Railway had received a small box from Retford addressed to a Mr William Town of Sorby Street, Sheffield. When the recipient, a young man, opened the box, he was shocked to find it contained the dead body of a female child. A note was in the box which read: 'Well, William I have sent you this box and I hope you will carefully examine it and put it away respectfully as you have behaved so badly towards me. By the time you get this box I will have left Retford and I hope never to see you again. It died as it was born. You are the cause of all my misery but I hope that God will provide something for me. You will never prosper. I have sent many letters but you won't even answer them. You promised me money.' The note, which was badly written and barely intelligible, had no signature attached. On finding what was in the box, Mr Town alerted the police and the body was taken away to await a coroners' inquest. (Vickers, J.E., *The Unseen, the Unsightly and the Amusing*, 1997)

JANUARY 14TH

1832: At a meeting of the town council this morning, Mr Hurst of Doncaster presented the plans for the proposed extension to the Town Hall. The present building, which holds the session house as well as the prison, is admittedly bad, being inadequate for the public and the safe custody of prisoners. The main extension will be to the present session house, which is estimated to cost between £3,000 and £4,000. It also means that a proportion of an existing yard will have to be built over and the new session house will abut onto the houses on Castle Green. Inevitably this means shutting out all the light and air except for the roof, but it is felt that the extra room would make this acceptable. By this extension it was hoped that the inhabitants would have a place to hold public meetings, the magistrates could carry on their course of justice and the police could safely lodge all disturbers of public peace.

The town trustees were willing to give £1,000 towards the extension and it is estimated that public subscription would raise the rest. (*Sheffield Independent*)

January 15th

1774: Today an advertisement for the sale of silk mill, which was later to become the Sheffield workhouse on Kelham Street, was inserted in the local newspaper:

Sale of lease Wm Bower bankrupt at Sheffield:

The large and extensive five storey Building extending over several acres with one of the compleatest [*sic*] of Silk Mills in this Kingdom. The building includes a good dwelling house, several Offices and a spacious Gardens etc. The Silk Mills are in a very good state of Repair and still employ a great number of Women and Children. The building has been made useful at a vast Expense which must make this Purchase a very desirable one indeed. The owners of the premises having spent within a few Years at least £7,000 to repair and rebuild additional buildings. The sale includes the whole of that curious Machinery known by the Name of KELHAM WHEELS which is used for grinding and glazing the cutlery.

The mill was built in 1758 by a Mr Middleton and was converted into a cotton mill by Mr Joseph Wells and Thomas Heathfield. (Leader, R., *Sheffield Local Directory*, Sheffield Independent Press, 1830)

JANUARY 16TH

1880: An account of the suffering of one impoverished family in Sheffield was revealed at the inquest on the body of Mary Good, who lodged on Alma Street. She had been deserted by her husband many years previously, and was since supported only by her children. On January 5th, she obtained a ticket requesting the workhouse medical officer attend her as she was suffering from dropsy. He ordered her to go into the workhouse as she could not receive proper food or attention where she was, but she refused to go. Finally relenting on January 10th she went to the workhouse by cab, which the workhouse authorities had agreed to pay for. Within five minutes of entering the door, having been removed from the cab by chair (as she was unable to walk), she was dead. The eldest of her sons, William (13), told the coroner that he and his two little sisters sold matches and newspapers for a living and they generally earned about 5*d* a day. At weekends they might earn 7*d*, but their lodgings cost 6*d* a night, so they had little money for food. A verdict was given of death aggravated by want. (*Sheffield Independent*)

JANUARY 17TH

1882: A newspaper gave an account of a brutal attack on the Salvation Army on the previous day. The Army had 'put on its armour' at the Thomas Street barracks ready for its 'triumphant march' through the town at 1.30 p.m. Prior to that, the streets were crowded to watch what was advertised as 'mounted officers and a brass band with female trumpeters led by General Booth commanding it'. This announcement roused a lot of curiosity and the parade, headed by General and Mrs Booth, set off at the allotted time and progressed along Broomhall Street, Fitzwilliam Street and Regent Street. The Army is accustomed to hecklers and insults but they were unprepared for the stone throwing, mud slinging and blasphemous threats directed at them. Hooting and yelling mobs surrounded the carriages as they reached the Albert Hall where, finally, they were able to escape at the greatest possible speed. Once inside, the General and all the other officers had some refreshments and the proceedings ended with General Booth leading them in prayers. Despite the hostility they had received that day, he assured the crowd that the Army was increasing in Sheffield. (*Sheffield Evening Star*)

January 18th

1840: At about 4 a.m., an abandoned female child was found by two men who were going to their work upon Little Sheffield Bridge, situated on South Street, Sheffield Moor. The child was placed in a doorway in a small rush basket, akin with that of a painter's basket used for carrying brushes. The child was dressed in a flannel binder, a cotton shirt, flannel petticoat, and white cotton gown. Her outer garments consisted of a plum-coloured cloak and plum-coloured silk bonnet lined with yellow calico and she was wrapped in an old green baize table cover, which was much stained with ink. The age of the child was estimated to have been two to three months and she appeared well-fed and healthy. The child was taken to Mr Drake, the constable, and then later removed to the workhouse. 'If anyone recognizes the clothing of the child or who can give such information as may lead to the apprehension and conviction of the unfeeling Parent shall received a Reward of Two Pounds on application to Benjamin Slater Union clerk to the Guardians, Sharrow Cottage. Dated 18 January 1840.' (*Sheffield Independent*)

JANUARY 19TH

1794: On this day (which was Queen Anne's birthday), the Sheffield Loyal Independent Volunteers showed their support by parading through the principal streets of the town. Firing a volley of shots at intervals, they halted outside the Tontine Inn, where they made a further three discharges of their rifles. Assembling themselves into a ring, one of the Volunteers stepped into the middle to sing 'God Save the King'. Windows, balconies and roofs in the area were occupied by spectators, including the Duke of Norfolk, who later gave 20 guineas to the men to drink Her Majesty's health. The men were led by Major Althorpe, who, the following year, was promoted to Lieutenant Colonel. Originally, they had grey uniforms but later changed them to scarlet tunics. The following day it was reported in the *Sheffield Courant*: 'Our readers will be candid enough to excuse the delay in publication of this week's paper there being a stoppage of all business in the office yesterday as most of the men employed herein belong to the Volunteer Corps'. The badge of the Volunteer had an emblem of a set of cymbals and a tambourine engraved on it. It goes without saying that the day of celebration ended with a feast. (*Sheffield Courant*)

January 20th

1870: This evening an annual Christmas entertainment was given at the St Joseph's Reformatory Home for Girls on Howard Hill. The *Sheffield Independent* reported that: 'The sisters of the institution started the proceedings with an animated play entitled "The Chinese Mother". The plot revolved around the mission of China and was of an instructive nature to the audience. The play was watched with interest by the girls and friends of the institution and was followed by refreshments provided by the sisters and inmates. The public are doubtlessly aware that a recent fund has been started to enable the sisters to send a few girls to Canada or other colonies. For a trifling sum of money to pay the passage money and an outfit of clothes a Government Agent dispatches the girl to a place of service. This could not fail to recommend itself in as much as the poor children were thereby removed from their old associations of crime and poverty. It was hoped that each child will have a fresh start in life and a career of honest industry. Sister Stephanie gratefully acknowledged the receipt of £32 from many kind friends. She was grateful for similar contributions to be paid either to herself or to any of the committee members'. (*Sheffield Independent*)

JANUARY 21ST

1851: On this day, William Blount of Sheffield had a very narrow escape from death. He had just started his shift at Messrs H. & W. Turner's Fire Iron manufactory in Bridge Street, where he was employed oiling the machines. In order to do this, he had to mount a turning lathe to grease a horizontal shaft that ran along the top of one of the machines. Just as he had started, and, without any warning, the key of the coupling box caught his shirt and drew him twice around the shaft. Screaming in agony, his workmates were unable to help him as the shaft then threw him onto the floor, leaving him clothed in only his stockings and neckerchief. Thankfully, he escaped from the incident relatively unscathed, but his shirt, waistcoat and trousers were torn to shreds. Fortunately, being made of cheap material, his clothes did not hold together, or he would have instantly been killed. Mr Blount is reported to have been dreadfully bruised on various parts of his body, particularly on his head, which struck against the floor of the room above. Had it been a bottom instead of a top shaft, it was thought that death would have been inevitable. (*Sheffield Independent*)

January 22nd

1862: On this day, many newspaper columns detailed an account of a robbery. Some workmen, passing the shop of Mr Sharp, watchmaker and jewellers, about seven o'clock on the morning of January 21st discovered that a pane of glass was broken. They roused Mr Sharp by banging loudly on the back door leading to his living quarters. Upon investigation, it was found that a number of jet ornaments and, in fact, every article within an arms length of the broken pane had been stolen. Fortunately, the proprietor of the shop was in the habit of removing the more valuable items of jewellery every night and thus a much more serious loss was avoided. As the loss amounted to between £4 and £5, a constable was called for and investigations were undertaken; several suspects were questioned. It seems probable that the robbery was affected about 3 a.m., for near that time a person who lived on the other side of the street was roused by the noise of breaking glass. Unfortunately he did not investigate the sound, nor give any alarm. (*Sheffield Times*)

January 23rd

1829: It was announced that a young boy (13) who had gone missing had been recovered safe and returned back to his parents. In June of last year, the *Sheffield Iris* noted the disappearance of the boy, William Hilliard, after returning home from school. His parents told him to change his suit for a more inferior one and he was wearing this suit when he disappeared from his parents' house at Heeley. A description of the boy stated that he was 'low set and pale looking' and his parents were of 'respectable circumstances and the boy himself heir to some property'. It seems that the father had travelled many miles in the hope of finding his son. The previous week, as a consequence of a tip-off, he had travelled to Uttoxeter, where he found him in the company of a set of chimneysweeps, amongst whom attempts had been made to barter the boy for a guinea. The father was so pleased that he brought the boy into the office. In the six months the child had been missing, his father stated that 'he had subsisted by a variety of juvenile expedients the probability of which his appearance by no means disparaged'. (*Sheffield Iris*)

JANUARY 24TH

1846: On this day, Madame Ablamowicz's farewell concert was announced at the Music Hall, which was expected to be 'one of the most brilliant we ever had in this town'. The *Sheffield Independent* reported that: 'Anxious to render her concert still more worthy of support, she had engaged the services of the well-known London vocalist, Miss A. Romer of the Royal Academy of Music. Miss Romer is, at present, singing to overflowing salons in Liverpool, Manchester and the principal towns of Lancashire and has proved an enormous success. The programme presents a variety of vocal and instrumental music of unsurpassed excellence. The lovers of music speak with raptures of Madame Ablamowicz's singing on the evening of January 10th this year at St Phillips Church, where she sang in aid of the choir fund'. The newspaper predicted that 'such is her popularity that we foretell a crowded audience, which will act not only as compensation for her spirited exertions but also as a parting tribute of the respect the town shows towards the lady's enormous talent. We most heartily wish her a fond farewell and the knowledge that if she should grace us once more with her presence the town will once again show their appreciation in their usual manner'. (*Sheffield Independent*)

January 25th

1831: Today, Hugh Parker Esq. and other magistrates on the bench instructed the constables to apprehend all vagrants and persons begging in the streets and take them to the workhouse. There they were to be given the usual accommodation of supper, bed (straw) and breakfast. In making the orders, the magistrates stated that inhabitants of the town had justly complained of the number of sturdy beggars who had threatened the poor and timid (the evils of public begging had been on the increase during the last two years). The numbers of fraudulent beggars parading the streets of Sheffield during the last summer and autumn was highly discreditable to the police authorities. Some of the beggars were attended by women and children, who sang hymns and spiritual songs whilst collecting pennies. Another class of beggar seen on the streets were men dressed in threadbare clothes and having on a white apron, claiming to be 'unfortunate tradesman'. Both types of swindlers were reaping a rich harvest, particularly on a Saturday night. It was worthy of remark that most mistaken benefactors to these vagrants are females. Those claiming to be beggars during the day were seen buying spirituous liquors the same night. (*Sheffield Courant*)

JANUARY 26TH

1863: A report was given on the state of trade in Sheffield, which read: 'Considering the period of the year, and the critical position of affairs in America, the iron trade in this town is in a far more satisfactory position that at any other similar period for years past. The demand for iron bars is still only moderate, but to replace that we have several active enquiries about rails and railway ironwork generally. Should only a portion of the proposed new lines and extensions receive Parliament's sanction, there is no doubt but that there will be a very large demand for railway ironwork for the new lines. We are aware that orders for ironwork for the new stations will be on the increase which will keep the mills and forges of Sheffield busy for some time to come. The steel trade is also improving, and there is reason to believe that there will be a considerable improvement next spring as orders have been received in all departments of the steel industry. It is believed from these improvements that Sheffield could look forward to a more prosperous year than that of 1862, when there was an economic depression which affected all trades'. (*Sheffield Times*)

JANUARY 27TH

1830: The *Sheffield Courant* today reported that: 'Sheffield is, at present, experiencing one of the harshest winters for some years'. On Wednesday, January 27th, as the Wellington coach was on its way to Sheffield from Derbyshire, the driver saw two men lying by the wayside completely overcome by the severity of the weather. One was so weakened that he had lain down in the snow and he would most certainly have perished had the coach not arrived so opportunely. The other man was barely able to stand and they were both taken to Castleton hospital. The Hope coach from London was unable to get any further than Penistone, where they were forced to remain for the night. The following day, it set off for Sheffield, the journey taking four hours, although the distance was only 26 miles. All lines of communication between Sheffield and Hull via Thorne were closed. The previous night and later on in the day on the 27th, the snow continued to fall and, complete with a sharp frost, it was intensely cold. The thermometer in Nelson Street in the centre of the city of Sheffield standing at 27 degrees Fahrenheit. (*Sheffield Courant*)

January 28th

1840: An inquest was held on the body of James Hill, a man who was employed by the surveyor of Brightside Highways, at Mr Ashmore's public house in Brightside before the coroner, Mr T. Badger. Hill had been found in the river near the Brightside Paper Mills and it appears in evidence that the last time he was seen was in Willey Street, Wicker. It is not known how he got into the water, but witnesses said that he was quite sober, and he was, at the time, making a survey of the streets around Brightside as part of his employment. The jury returned a verdict of 'found drowned', although they had no doubt that as a consequence of the want of fencing to the river up to the end of Willey Street, the poor man had probably fallen into the water and been carried down by the flood to the place where he was found. The jury therefore expressed a strong opinion on the impropriety of the place remaining any longer in its present state. It was known that three persons had drowned there in four years. (*Sheffield Times*)

JANUARY 29TH

1828: A fascinatingly gruesome event was reported today in the *Sheffield Independent*: 'Mr Marriot of Attercliffe had lately had at his farm in Orgreave a fine heifer, which he had bought at the market several months previously. Curiously the same heifer died under the following singular circumstances. The animal became sickly and after lingering for about three months died in a state of great exhaustion. It was discovered that the whole carcass contained hardly any blood whatever. After its death, the medical men were surprised to find upon opening it up to ascertain the cause of its death, an adder upwards of a yard long within its head, just emerging from the larynx. The reptile was dead, but from the fresh appearance of its skin it was evident that it had been swallowed by the calf at the commencement of its illness, and must have been alive in the stomach until within a few hours of the death of the heifer.' The medical men stated their astonishment that the reptile could have survived so long within the body of the heifer and that such an occurrence had been unknown to them previously. (*Sheffield Independent*)

January 30th

1850: It was reported in the newspapers that, on the previous evening, the celebrated Shakespearian actor William Charles Macready made his farewell appearance at Sheffield to a crowded theatre. Every box was full and even the orchestra was filled with visitors. After performing *Richelieu* (written by Edward Bulwer Lytton) in splendid style, Mr Macready was called for with the strongest demonstration of enthusiasm and when he re-appeared a great part of the audience rose to give him a parting cheer. He told them: 'I would not trespass upon your patience with the ceremony of formal leave taking, but where I have been favoured during the course of my theatrical career with much liberal patronage – and where there will also exist for me associations of deepest interest – I may perhaps be excused for the desire to offer you at least my parting acknowledgements and to embody sincerest good wishes in the word, as I bid you in my professional capacity, most gratefully and respectfully a last farewell.' A desire had been expressed that he remain in the town for another performance, but his list of engagements made it impossible. He left Sheffield on the morning of January 30th to perform at his next venue in Nottingham. (*Sheffield Post*)

JANUARY 31ST

1841: An account was published on the subject of some daring villains who had affected an entrance into the house of James Hallam, a grocer of Ecclesall Road, on the previous evening. It seems that these miscreants had gained their entrance through the window of the front bed chamber over the shop. All the inmates of the house were in a back room for most of the evening and the crime was not discovered till half past eleven. Upon retiring, Mrs Hallam found the window open, the chamber ransacked and twelve £5 notes and 35 sovereigns taken from a box. As far as can be ascertained, the robbery had been executed early in the evening, since the window was observed to be open at about eight o'clock. The window of the house of Mr George Wigfall, which was next door, was opened at the same time but for some reason – perhaps a disturbance – nothing was taken. Since the breaking up of the notorious gang, some of whom were convicted at the Doncaster Sessions, these evening robberies had ceased. It then emerged that they had resumed, and readers of the *Sheffield Independent* were advised to carefully examine their property. (*Sheffield Independent*)

FEBRUARY 1ST

1893: On this day it became known that the town of Leeds had applied for city status, and the Mayor of Sheffield called a town council meeting to send in their own application to the Home Office. In the petition, the town clerk emphasized the historic and industrial development of a town with more than 300,000 people. The Mayor's enthusiasm was not entirely shared by the rest of the councillors. Alderman William Smith admitted that the Mayor had asked him to second the proposition but he had refused to do so, 'because he did not feel himself sufficiently interested in the matter'. Alderman Brittain, who did agree with the resolution, told the council that he thought it was desirable to aspire to the dignity of a city but he agreed with Smith that there was not much in it. Alderman Bradley was not aware that there was such widespread feeling in the town in favour of this proposal. On February 7th, Sir Godfrey Lushington wrote to the town clerks of both Leeds and Sheffield to say that the Queen had accepted both recommendations, and they both would be awarded the status of cities. (Walton, M., *Sheffield: Its Story and its Achievements,* Sheffield, Amethyst Press, 1984)

FEBRUARY 2ND

1877: On this day, the newspapers carried a report about cooking lessons in Sheffield schools. A woman named Mrs Greenup, who had started to give cooking lessons at Crookesmoor School, was sent by the Sheffield School Board for training at the South Kensington School of Cookery. Local MP Mr Mundella attended the school and found Mrs Greenup giving instruction to a class of forty-eight girls. The class was taught in two parts: a lecture began the lesson, and a demonstration followed. February 1st was designated as 'cold meat day', where preparations of palatable ways of serving cold meat were explored. Mrs Greenup showed the girls how to prepare 'hash' and the girls took notes of ingredients and how to prepare it. Later, Mr Mundella asked the girls if they had used any of the lessons to make meals at home, and about a third of the class raised their hands. He spoke of the need for girls to be able to cook well, and how to economize to make the ingredients go further. He pointed out that, being girls, they probably would not earn their living by cooking such food, but they would perhaps be able to make their home happy and comfortable. (*Sheffield Evening Star*)

FEBRUARY 3RD

1900: This morning a man was brought into the Sheffield Court for collecting bogus subscriptions for a man who had recently died. John Gallagher (19), of Browns Yard, Sheffield, was charged with obtaining money by false pretences on different dates in January. On January 3rd, the prisoner came into Mr Pearson's shop wishing him to subscribe towards the funeral of a man named Joseph Shaw, who had died a few days previously. The prisoner had a subscription list with about a dozen names written on it and the alleged amount of subscriptions given. Mr Pearson knew Shaw and so he gave the man 2s. Gallagher then went into the fish market and asked the same from Mr H. Wainwright, and then he went around all the customers in the shop collecting money. Elizabeth Shaw, the wife of the dead man, stated that she never received any subscriptions and she did not need them as she had sufficient money to bury her husband. The prisoner, who did not appear to realise the serious nature of the charge, said that he spent the money on drink. Despite offering to refund the money, he was sentenced to prison for twenty-eight days. (*Sheffield Independent*)

FEBRUARY 4TH

1834: An inquest was held on the bodies of a husband and wife today; they had both burned to death. The inquest was held at the vestry room of the Sheffield workhouse before the coroner, Mr Badger. The chief constable gave the details to the coroner and the jury. It seems that the couple, who had lived at Snow Hill, Park, were Mr John Rose and his wife Ann. On the previous Monday morning, Mrs Rose was sweeping up the hearth in the kitchen when her clothes accidentally caught fire. On attempting to extinguish the flames, she set the bedclothes on fire, which her husband was lying on. He had been paralyzed and confined to bed, which had been in the kitchen for the last three years. Before any assistance could be obtained, nearly the whole of the bed and other articles of furniture were consumed. Mr and Mrs Rose were so badly burnt that although medical attention had been called, they remained in great pain until they both died in the early hours of the following morning, within an hour of each other. The coroner summed up the evidence for the jury, who brought in a verdict of accidental death. (*Sheffield Iris*)

FEBRUARY 5TH

1858: This evening, a case was heard of a sweet shop being used for gambling by several young boys, encouraged by the proprietor, Mr John Henry. It seems that PC Wood was passing the shop the previous Saturday when he observed a number of boys inside. Peering through the window, he saw Mr Henry at a table holding a bag in which there were pieces of wood with numbers on. The boys paid money and then were allowed to draw a number out of the bag. If they won, they were served sweets by Mrs Henry. The policeman told the magistrate that there were between eight and ten boys in the shop, ranging from ten to sixteen years of age. The magistrate told Mr Henry: 'It is most abominable that you should carry on such a trade. You could not do anything more objectionable. You are debauching the minds and ruining this rising generation by teaching and encouraging them to gamble.' He was fined 5s and told to pay 4s costs, but when he told the magistrate that he didn't have a penny to pay the costs he was told, 'then a warrant will be issued against your goods'. (*Sheffield Times*)

FEBRUARY 6TH

1882: An inquest was held into the death of a soldier, George Baker, who had committed suicide. Sergeant William Power Lane identified the body of the man, who was a driver in the Royal Artillery. He told the coroner that he had known the deceased for about three and a half years. During that time Baker had never complained of being in bad health, he was not in disgrace, nor was he a man of intemperate habits. He had seen him on the Tuesday before and he seemed in good spirits. Another driver, Thomas Blower, stated that the deceased was his assistant and had helped him with the horses. He had left Baker in the stables at 9.40 a.m. on Friday morning and when he returned an hour later found him hanging from a hook. Blower immediately cut the man down but he was already dead. William Thompson, gunner, suggested that the reason might have been about another soldier who had hung himself in the barracks a short time ago. A verdict was recorded was that Baker had committed suicide whilst in a state of temporary insanity. (*Yorkshire Post*)

FEBRUARY 7TH

1876: The *Sheffield Independent* reported that the 'Cabman's Rest' in Glossop Road was completed. The building, which was made of wood and glass, had seats running on three sides. It could hold ten cabmen and was described as a 'very cosy, sightly little place'. In the centre of the rest lay a stove, which was specially designed by Messrs Butler of Liverpool. It occupied very little space but gave out great heat, also affording facilities for cooking. At the end of the rest was a sink with all the appliances necessary for washing. The plans for the rest were drawn up by Messrs Flockton and Abbott (architects) and the water company fitted all of the pipes and fittings free of charge. The Revd R. Stainton was thanked on behalf of the cabmen, due to his efforts to secure for them this very desirable accommodation. The want of such shelters in other parts of the town would now be felt more keenly than before. (*Sheffield Independent*)

FEBRUARY 8TH

1858: An inquest into the deaths of three people killed in a firework explosion on Scotland Street was held today. After being sworn in, the jury saw the badly burned bodies at the workhouse. The bodies had been found in the wreckage of a shop belonging to Mr Thomas Corbridge. The victims were Mr Bywater, Mrs Corbridge and Mrs Walker. It seems that Mr Bywater had been making fireworks for the Adelphi Theatre. The explosion happened at about 12.20 p.m., shaking the house and several buildings around it. The jury returned a verdict that all three had been killed by an explosion of fireworks, but of the cause of the explosion there was no satisfactory evidence. The coroner stated that there should be some regulation adopted by the Town Council for preventing the manufacture of fireworks in such a built-up area. (*Sheffield Free Press*)

FEBRUARY 9TH

1568: A triple marriage was performed on this day, securing the two houses of Cavendish and Talbot. George Talbot, the sixth Earl of Shrewsbury, rose to power under Queen Elizabeth I – becoming a member of the Privy Council and Lieutenant-General for Yorkshire, Nottinghamshire and Derbyshire. After the execution of Thomas, Duke of Norfolk in 1572, he also became the Earl Marshall of England. At the wedding, George married Bess of Hardwick and her eldest son, Henry Cavendish, married George's daughter, Lady Grace Talbot. Bess of Hardwick's youngest daughter, Mary, also married Gilbert Talbot. By the forging of this triple alliance, the family thus owned large estates in Yorkshire, Nottinghamshire, Derbyshire and Shropshire, as well as other properties in Staffordshire, Herefordshire, Oxfordshire, Cheshire, Wiltshire, Leicestershire, Gloucestershire and London. Talbot also owned castles at Sheffield, Pontefract and Tutbury, a large manor house at South Wingfield, hunting lodges at Sheffield, Tutbury and Worksop, the former Rufford Abbey, a house by the baths at Buxton, and a small lodge at Handsworth beyond Sheffield Park. He rebuilt the lodge at Worksop into a fine country house and for a time owned the new hall in the park at Tankersley. He also converted the monastic buildings at Rufford into a desirable turret house renamed Manor Lodge. (Hey, D., *A History of Sheffield*, Carnegie Publishing Ltd, 1998)

FEBRUARY 10TH

1849: The announcement was made that the new railway line from Sheffield to Brighton would open to the public on the following Monday. This portion of the line measured around 7¼ miles in length, and the industrial works upon were the heaviest in the eastern section of this railway. It commenced at Bridgehouses station with its immense 660-yard long viaduct, crossing the Wicker, the River Dun and the canal. The line ran over embankments and through cuttings alternately, descending generally at the rate of one in 150 to the Handsworth tunnel, which was 374 yards long. From the Handsworth tunnel, the line descends by a similar gradient of 1 in 150 to its junction with the Midland Railway. The stations on this part of the line are at Darnall, 2½ miles from the town, and at Beighton. The viaduct cost £80,000 per mile and the cost of the works on the other part of the line were around £18,000 per mile. Work on the railway line commenced in October 1846, and the viaduct in May 1847. In later years, it would prove be of enormous value to passengers travelling south, as previously they would have to travel to Masbrough, Rotherham to catch trains to Chesterfield, London and elsewhere. (Bunker, B., *Portrait of Sheffield*, Hale Publishing, 1972)

FEBRUARY 11TH

1846: On this day an inquest was held on the death of Mr John Riley (30), a pianoforte tuner, at the Cutler's Arms on Fargate. On Monday night, the young man returned to the house of his mother-in-law just after 10 p.m. He had been giving lessons to the daughters of Mr Vinor of West Street. After eating two roast potatoes, he retired to bed. His dead body was found by his mother-in-law the following morning. It seems that for some time he had not been on speaking terms with both his mother and father, who disapproved of his manner of earning a living. He had, a few days before, informed his father that he was supplementing his income by playing the piano at a public house on Saturday and Sunday nights, and both of his parents stopped speaking to him on account of this. The surgeon, Mr Wild, was called and found the young man lying on his left side with his knees drawn up to his abdomen. The post-mortem revealed that he had a defect on the right side of the heart. The jury therefore returned a verdict of death through natural causes. (*Sheffield Independent*)

FEBRUARY 12TH

1790: On this day, a number of punishments were recorded: nine men were put in the stocks for tippling in a public house during Divine Service, and two boys were made to do penance in church for playing at trip during Divine Service. They were punished by having to stand in the middle of the church during the service with their trip sticks erect. (Leader, R., *Sheffield Local Directory*, Sheffield Independent Press, 1830)

———•◆•———

1805: It was resolved today that better accommodation was wanted for the magistrates acting in this populous District of the Riding, and that a secure prison was required for temporary confinement and safe custody of felons and disorderly persons. In order to do this it was further:

Resolved: that a meeting be convened before the 26th instant in order to consider the best mode of carrying the above resolution into effect.

Resolved: that Vincent Eyre Esq. be invited to attend this meeting to transmit the resolution to His Grace the Duke of Norfolk with a humble hope that His Grace would take the same into consideration and promote an undertaking which appears to be for the good of the town.

Resolved that a committee of respectable men be formed to look into such accommodation and report back to the meeting.

(Leader, J.D., *Records of the Burgery of Sheffield*, Sheffield Independent Press, 1897)

FEBRUARY 13TH

1841: On this day, a woman named Francis Wragg (44) was charged with uttering (passing on) two counterfeit shillings and two counterfeit sixpences in Sheffield. It was reported that Wragg had gone into an eating house owned by a Mrs Sarah Hill in Commercial Street and had purchased some small articles, which she paid for with a shilling. She later returned to the eating house and bought further items, for which she paid over a sixpence. Foolishly returning to the same place for the third time, she paid for several articles amounting to 1/6 d. The owner of the eating house had by this time realised that the two coins which she had been given were false and called the constables. It was later stated by a jeweller and watchmaker that all the coins were false. When Wragg was questioned by the police, she told them that she was a seller of nuts and oranges and that she had received the coins following the sales of these items. She was arrested and sent for trial at the next assizes. Wragg appeared at the York Assizes on Wednesday, March 10th, 1841, where she was given a six-month prison sentence. (*Sheffield Telegraph*)

February 14th

1846: A meeting took place of the Market Commission today, to consider the proposal of the Duke of Norfolk to enlarge and improve the present market accommodation. Plans had been prepared by Messrs Weightman and Hadfield, which were laid before the commission. It was suggested that, by demolishing the Tontine property, a space would be available to provide a covered market of approximately 100 yards long by 40 yards wide. The new market would have a frontage onto the Haymarket with entrances on each side and ends. It was obvious that if this design were carried out, it would be the most complete measure of improvements which Sheffield had ever witnessed. Speaking on behalf of the Duke, Mr Ellison requested any hints on the subject from the Commission and the fullest explanations were entered into. In the event of the Tontine site being adopted for the market, the present vegetable market on King Street and Castle Street would make an excellent site for the Council Hall and Bankruptcy Court. If this was agreed, it was thought that the Corporation might purchase this site from His Grace on more favourable terms than a private individual. (*Sheffield Times*)

FEBRUARY 15TH

1870: A meeting of the Sheffield Emigration Committee took place at the Royal George Hotel. They had been convened to enquire into the case of William Broadhead, who had received funds from the committee to emigrate to America with his family. A week earlier he had returned to Sheffield, as he was unable to find work. The meeting was chaired by Revd J.F. Witty, who stated that he should have looked for work elsewhere. He had been promised a job by a cousin working in Philadelphia in a saw mill, but a day or so prior to his arrival the post was cancelled. Broadhead appeared in front of the committee and assured them that he had tried to find work. After considerable discussion, to which the committee freely expressed their opinions both for and against Broadhead, it was suggested that he repay the subscriptions, but no one could agree. Finally, it was decided that he be allowed to keep the money, but so bitter was the disagreement that two of the committee resigned on the spot and Mr Wright informed the rest of the committee that they would no longer be able to use his house as a place to hold their meetings. (*Sheffield Independent*)

FEBRUARY 16TH

1856: On this day was printed an account of a robbery which had taken place the previous Saturday. Mr Edward Overton, mason and builder of Little Sheffield, went out with his wife, leaving three young children in bed at about 8 p.m. On their return, at about 10 p.m., they found that their house had been entered by thieves, who had stolen two hams left hanging in the kitchen, about £32 in money, a silk dress, a coat and six silver teaspoons. One of the children, a little girl, was disturbed by the sound of voices and thought that her parents had returned. Shortly afterwards, she heard a footstep on the stairs and from the room where she lay, she saw a strange man and woman enter the front bedroom. She was frightened but made no noise. The man and the woman, who was without a bonnet, ransacked the upper room and afterwards remained some time below, no doubt examining the chiffonier and dresser, which were also found to be completely ransacked. The thieves, who in all probability lived somewhere in the immediate vicinity, had left the house no more than a few minutes before the return of Mr and Mrs Overton. (*Sheffield Times*)

FEBRUARY 17TH

1871: A meeting was held in the Mayor's Parlour to discuss the expediency of establishing an institution for the training of nurses for the sick. Mr Jonathon Barber referred to the great difficulty that was felt by families afflicted by sickness in securing competent and trusty nurses. Having their origins in Miss Nightingale, there had sprung up in London, Liverpool and Birmingham, as well as other parts of the country, institutions which had been extremely successful in the support and management of nurses. He had made a partial canvass amongst his friends, the result of which was a list of donations amounting to £350. Mr Barber estimated that to commence the scheme they would need about £600 of capital and £250 of annual income. He stated that he would be happy to place the results of his efforts in the hands of such ladies and gentlemen who were disposed to take up the idea. Dr Sale moved that it was desirable to establish such an institution in Sheffield. The motion was unanimously agreed to and a committee appointed, with Mr Barber appointed as secretary. It was hoped that many ladies of the town would respond to this cause. (*Sheffield Post*)

FEBRUARY 18TH

1863: In today's newspapers it was reported that a former Inspector of Sheffield police had been found dead in New York. Mr Samuel Linley had retired from the police force, and, a few weeks previously, had emigrated with his family to the United States. The family had visited New York on January 24th, Mr Linley having some business in the city. However, not arriving back at the time expected, his protracted absence caused his family considerable alarm, and apprehensions were manifested for his safety. A search was begun, which failed to give any clue to his whereabouts. On Monday, the fears of his family were realized by the startling announcement of his death in one of the New York papers. From the scant information received, it would appear that the poor man was picked up in the street in a state of insensibility and removed to a neighbouring hospital. Unfortunately, Mr Linley never rallied and died within three hours of his admission. Death is supposed to have resulted from injuries sustained from a fall, which hypotheses are favoured by the proximity of a flight of stone stairs, at the foot of which he was found. The deceased was fifty-three years of age. (*Sheffield Independent*)

FEBRUARY 19TH

1848: On this day, a newspaper printed a most disturbing report on a woman who gave birth to conjoined twins: 'LUSUS NATUREA. One of those rare, but to the feelings of parties most interested, very painful occurrences happened last week in the practice of Mr William Askam of Shalesmoor. A woman gave birth to twins, which are joined together from the upper part of the breast bone to the navel, and, of course, their natural position is to lie nearly face to face. One is a male; but the sex of the other is doubtful. The figures of both are as well developed as children usually are when a little short of the usual period before birth; and they were certainly alive a short time before they were born. We cannot of course detail the minute appearances presented on dissection, as they would not interest our general readers; but we understand the internal organs are complete as for two children, with some curious ramification and deviations from the usual structure; and that the most important organs are far more completely developed in one of the children than the other. The mother has recovered from the birth and we are told she is rapidly returning back to full health'. (*Yorkshire Post*)

FEBRUARY 20TH

1858: As a result of the industrial distress among the working classes, Miss Roberts of Park Grange announced with characteristic liberality her arrangements to distribute 300 quarts of soup to 500 poor people. It was expected that the soup would be distributed to people residing in the Park, Dyers Hill, St Paul's, St Mary's and the Wicker districts over the next four weeks. The first distribution was made on Wednesday at the school room, South Street, Park. It was intended that the soup would be distributed every Wednesday and Friday, until the industrial distress was relieved. Since Miss Roberts announced her intention, and, through the generosity of several gentlemen, the amount of soup given out was increased to 950 quarts of first-rate, quality ingredients. A boiler had been erected especially for the manufacture of the soup and the management is entrusted to Messrs Charlesworth and Coggin. Miss Roberts requested that donations of vegetables or meat will be gladly received for use in the soup at the School room on South Street. She also asked for any lady who could assist her in the task to put forward their name for her consideration. (*Sheffield Independent*)

February 21st

1798: On this day, a meeting was held at the Cutler's Hall for the purpose of starting a subscription list for the defence of the country, and a general muster of the Sheffield Loyal Volunteer Corps. Major Althorp told the meeting that his troops had offered their personal services to the King in case of invasion or danger thereof. Major Althorp and his troop were thanked by the Mayor and he put forward a suggestion that if the Sheffield Volunteers were called out on active service, that a fund be raised to support any families who needed assistance during their absence. Major Althorp asked for volunteers to come forward to defend the town and its neighbourhood should the need arise. The meeting also agreed that the town of Sheffield would supply two troops of cavalry and four companies of infantry. Foot and carbine drill was to be held every Monday, Tuesday and Wednesday. All guns, ammunition and tunics were to be collected and given back to the Quartermaster after every drill. All the Volunteers had to be over seventeen years of age and of a height of no less than 5ft 6in, and chest measurements were not to be less than 32in. (*Sheffield Iris*)

FEBRUARY 22ND

1831: An inquest was held before Thomas Badger Esq., the Sheffield coroner, at the Bull and Mouth public house on the death of Mr John Beaver Mason, a builder of Shalesmoor. The jury proceeded to the house of the deceased, where his body was found with the throat cut and a razor nearby, the blade of which had been made firm to the handle with pack thread. Evidence was given which showed that, because of pecuniary matters, he had recently become melancholy and had exhibited on several occasions an aberration of mind. After hearing the summing up of the coroner, the jury returned a verdict that the deceased destroyed himself in an act of insanity. On the same day and same place, another inquest was held on the death of Ann Brassington, a six-year-old child. It was shown, to the satisfaction of the jury, that when playing with other children, the child fell down and badly cut herself with a tin can she was holding in her hand at the time, and death swiftly ensued. The jury brought in a verdict of accidental death. (*Sheffield Independent*)

February 23rd

1847: Today, many of the most eminent men of Sheffield signed the following Temperance Medical Certificate, which has been distributed throughout the town Compiled by the Temperance League, the certificates read:

We are of the opinion:

- That a very large portion of human misery, including poverty, disease and crime, is induced by the use of alcoholic or fermented liquors as beverages
- That the most perfect health is compatible with total abstinence from all such intoxicating beverages, whether in the form of ardent spirits, or as wine, beer, ale, porter, cider etc.
- That persons accustomed to such drinks may, with perfect safety, discontinue them entirely, either at once or gradually after a short time
- That total and universal abstinence from alcoholic liquors and intoxicating beverages of all sorts would greatly contribute to the health, the prosperity, the morality, and the happiness of the human race

Sixty-seven copies of the above certificate were sent out to medical practitioners of Sheffield and its neighbourhood, of which twenty-three were signed without reservation, six with modifications, four were returned unsigned and thirty-four were returned with no reply or explanation given. (Batty, S.R., *Sheffield,* Ian Allen, 1984)

February 24th

1856: This morning there was a tremendous explosion near the Arundel Street Gasometer between 11 a.m. and midday, which was placed on the corner of Earl Street. Half a dozen men in the employment of the gas company had been engaged in putting down some new pipes and valves, when William Hayes, the supervisor of the men, discovered there was an escape of gas. One of the men investigated with a lighted match and the explosion, which alarmed the whole neighbourhood, occurred. A small shed was demolished and some panes of glass broken in the windows of Arundel Street, and some of the men were buried in the debris. Two men, George Eyre of Effingham Street and John Blonk, who resided near the canal, were much injured about the head and had to be conveyed home in a cab. Patrick Flaherty and George Smith were not so badly injured that they had to leave their work. It was later found that the escaped gas had collected in the shed from a fractured joint under the wall. Fortunately for the workmen, the wall had been lifted straight up from its bed; had it been forced outwards, the consequences would have been much worse. (*Sheffield Free Press*)

FEBRUARY 25TH

1857: A garrotte robbery occurred in Occupation Road of Mr John Cocker. Although retired as senior partner, he liked to visit the works of John Cocker & Sons on the Wicker daily, returning home between 7 p.m. and 8 p.m. As he was passing between the end of Occupation Road and the Gardeners Arms public house, he noticed two men approaching him. One of them threw his arms around his neck so tightly that Cocker thought he was going to be strangled to death. He begged the men to take what they wanted as they threw him to the ground, and one of the ruffians held him with a foot on his throat whilst the other rifled his pockets. Suddenly, a man and woman approached, forcing the two men to flee, taking only 10s in silver with them. Mr Cocker was assisted to the Gardeners Arms and remained there whilst he recovered. He had a watch upon him which had not been found by the robbers. After a short while, he went back to the Town Hall, where he then gave information to the police. He informed officers that he had clearly seen the men as they pushed him to the ground, and so was able to give a good description of them. (*Sheffield Daily Telegraph*)

February 26th

1846: The shooting of an innkeeper was reported in the newspapers. On the morning of February 25th, two young men went into the Surrey Arms. Mr Greaves, the landlord, took exception to something they had said and one of them took from his pocket a pistol loaded with a ball, which he deliberately fired at Greaves' head. The ball entered Greaves' cheek on the right side. The villain who fired the pistol then made his escape. Upon hearing the explosion of the pistol, one of the landlord's male servants came to his assistance while the other young man commenced a violent attack upon Greave with a thick stick. Although he suffered several wounds to the back of his head, the servant succeeded in keeping hold of the man until the arrival of additional assistance. PC Crapper, the constable, was sent for and the man was handed over into his custody. Inspector Wakefield and several other officers went in search of the individual that had fired the pistol. In the course of a few hours he was found with the pistol re-loaded in his pocket. The prisoners gave their names as Joseph Hodkin and Joshua Eastwood when they were brought before the magistrate on February 26th. (*Sheffield Times*)

FEBRUARY 27TH

1830: Advertised in the *Sheffield Independent* today was the following advert, which showed the length of time it took to travel to Birmingham from Sheffield:

George Waddingham, grateful for the very liberal and extensive patronage already conferred on him, begs leave to acquaint Nobility, Gentry, Merchant, Manufacturers and the Public in general that he has for their better accommodation made arrangements for running a new and elegant four inside post coach called THE DEFIANCE.

The coach will travel to Birmingham in only nine hours every Morning (Mondays excepted) at Half-past Seven O Clock commencing on Tuesday next the 2nd March. The coach will travel by way of Baslow, Edensor, Chatsworth, Bakewell, Winster, Grange Mills, Ashbourne, Ellaston, Uttoxeter, Abbots Bromley, Rocester and Litchfield arriving at the CASTLE ALBION and GEORGE HOTELS in Birmingham by Half-past Four the same afternoon. THE DEFIANCE will leave the CASTLE ALBION and GEORGE HOTELS the next morning and arrive at the KINGS HEAD GENERAL COACH OFFICE, SHEFFIELD at Half-past four in time for all Coaches to the North. Particular attention will be paid to all Goods which will be delivered at a moderate charge, immediately on arrival of the Coach.

(Sheffield Independent)

FEBRUARY 28TH

1831: A poor Irish woman named Catherine Teeman was walking down the High Street, when, without any warning, she staggered into a shop run by a Mr Wooley. The woman was barely conscious and unable to understand anything that was said to her, so two watchmen were called, and, thinking that she was inebriated, she was taken to the Town Hall and put into one of the cells. In a short while, the constable, PC Bland, who was the keeper of the prison, became aware that the woman was actually ill and sent for a surgeon to look at her. Mr Needham arrived first and, after examining the poor creature, he stated that she laboured under an attack of apoplexy. By this time, Mr Knight, another surgeon, had arrived and both surgeons delivered all means of recovery they could; sadly, however, this was without success, and the woman was pronounced dead. After enquiries had been made in the town, relatives of the woman were found and they took her body away for burial. An inquest was held on Tuesday, March 1st, 1831 at the home of Mr Brown on Norfolk Street, the jury returning a verdict that she had 'died by a visitation from God'. (*Sheffield Iris*)

MARCH 1ST

1844: Mr Joseph Pitman made a visit to Sheffield to talk about phonography (shorthand) at the Cutler's Hall, in front of an overcapacity crowd. Mr Pitman began by stating that people were now living in an ever-changing age in which much had already been achieved. The changes which had taken place had accelerated very rapidly, but that development had not extended to the art of writing. It was thought that people ought to be able to express words onto paper as quickly as they would verbally. He had come to show a new method of communication by which writing was rendered as easy as speaking; in the English language, we have twenty-six letters and 50,000 words, but only twenty simple sounds, each of these having a single sign. He stated that to write 'Manchester', which contained ten letters, would require forty to forty-five strokes of the pen. While he repeated the name three times, his assistant, Mr Reid, wrote it seven times with phonography. He told the amazed crowds that 120 words a minute could be written by people skilled in this craft. He had witnessed his assistant writing 203 words a minute. Such was the interest in this novelty that when he finished his lecture, he received a spontaneous and warm applause. (*Sheffield Independent*)

MARCH 2ND

1874: Today's newspaper contained a report of a standing ovation which had been given to Mr Barry Sullivan at the Sheffield Theatre Royal the previous night. The pantomime season had finished and a reporter from the *Sheffield Independent* was pleased to state that the theatre had returned back to 'legitimate business' once more. The short season of tragedies began with *Hamlet*, which was played to a packed house. The pit was crowded and the gallery was full to overflowing, but the cramped audience fell into complete silence during the performance. Although Mr Sullivan was praised for his Hamlet, the reporter noted in his review that it was 'not in the same exalted category as his Richard III'. Mr Sullivan made his Hamlet a brave, relatively ordinary man, hardly the 'lunatic one minute and a craven loon the next' as was the case with the interpretation of some actors. He stated that 'the play was creditably put upon the stage. There was nothing remarkable in the way of scenery or effects but what there was effective and in good taste.' Mr Sullivan, who was at the time on a tour of West Riding theatres, was to proceed to Bradford on the following Monday. (*Sheffield Independent*)

MARCH 3RD

1862: On this day the trial of Thomas Slater (20) of Sheffield was heard at the York Assizes before Mr Justice Mellor. Slater was charged with causing the death of his mother, Harriet, on January 4th 1862. The court heard how he had been drinking with his mother when an altercation took place. It seems that she had borrowed a shilling from him and had refused to pay it back. In the beer house on West Bar, she went to strike her son with a poker but he hit her first with a savage blow to her mouth. At first she appeared to be unharmed, and continued to harangue her son. Shortly after the attack, however, her lip turned black, and, tragically, just after her return home, she passed away. The surgeon gave his opinion that the woman had died from the extravasations of blood on the brain caused by the blow. The jury found Slater guilty but recommended him to mercy due to the provocation from his mother. The judge, in summing up, stated that the prisoner ought never to have raised his hand towards his mother. If it had been anyone else, the judge would have ordered his discharge; as it was, he ordered him to be imprisoned with hard labour for two months. (*Sheffield Times*)

MARCH 4TH

1858: A report appeared today on a meeting by the Improvement Commissioners, which had taken place the previous evening. Mr Leader Junior asked why the street lamps were not on pillars instead of being attached on arms to the wall, as he had been assured that if they were mounted on pillars they would give more light. Mr Booth's answer was that they were usually mounted on walls to save the expense of pillars, and that the latter might cause an obstruction. Mr Leader suggested that perhaps a few could be erected on a trial basis to see if there was any improvement, which was agreed. The Cleansing Committee stated that they had not been able to obtain new places for urinals, but the surveyor was still in the process of trying to find a suitable place for them. Mr Booth asked, 'Why aren't the crossings cleared of snow?' and suggested that the unemployed poor might be set to the work. Mr Leader said that he had no authority over the paupers, and he did not expect them to work diligently unless a superintendent could be employed to watch them. Also, if they employed the poor, the committee would have to provide tools for them, which would prove to be an extra expense. (*Sheffield Independent*)

MARCH 5TH

1872: An inquest was held concerning the death of Richard Staniland, which had occurred at Shoreham Works, Bramall Lane a few days previously. Mr Nicholson, the owner of the works, stated that the deceased man had worked for him for four to five years as a wheelwright and he was forty-four years of age. Staniland was working on the morning of the incident, and one of his duties involved oiling the machinery. On this unfortunate occasion, a band had snapped and caught him round the head, dragging him into the machine. Mr Nicholson stated that if he had used proper precautions, the accident would not have happened. The coroner asked him whether it was the custom to stop the machinery whilst it was being oiled, and Mr Nicholson replied that he believed that it was not Staniland's custom to stop the machinery. A blacksmith employed at the same works told the jury that Staniland was working on the machinery when the accident happened, which tore off one of his legs and broke the other. The coroner said that he thought that no one was to blame for the accident but the unfortunate man himself. The jury returned a verdict of accidental death. (*Daily Telegraph*)

MARCH 6TH

1858: In the early hours of this morning, Isaac Dixon of the Minerva Tavern was found harbouring a night constable, Peter Rourke, on the premises of his public house when he should have been on duty. PC Moore stated that he had gone to the tavern at about 12.45 a.m. to see if he could hear any company still in the house, when he heard a voice which he recognised as being Rourke's. Both the front and back door were locked and so he rapped on the window, finally gaining entrance to the premises. The pub was in darkness, with the exception of one room. PC Moore challenged Dixon that he had other men in the house, and that he had heard Rourke's voice. Dixon denied it but when Moore demanded a candle to search the premises, Rourke emerged from a back room. Dixon stated that Rourke had just gone into the pub to light his lamp and hadn't been in the house a moment or two before Moore arrived. Chief constable Raynor told the Watch Committee that Rourke had admitted going into the house for a glass of ale and that the door had been fastened behind him. Dixon was fined 10*s* and costs. (*Sheffield Free Press*)

MARCH 7TH

1855: A lecture was given at the People's College on Thomas De Quincy, author of *Confessions of an Opium Eater*, by surgeon Mr Phillips. He began by explaining the effects of opium eating. He stated that: 'the appetite steals on the victim insensibly, but irresistibly; and wiles its charms with its wonderful visions. By a vast accumulation of imaginary power, it binds him in fetters he can never burst – fetters of agony. It gives an amazing, incredible development to the mental features and creates a sort of Elysium'. Mr Phillips then concentrated on the life story of Thomas De Quincy. He was born in Manchester on August 17th 1785, and, at the age of seventeen, he left home and went to London to seek his fortune. After several years, he attained a respectable position in employment. He confessed to first trying opium in 1804 to alleviate toothache and, at its zenith, the dose administered reached 8,000 drops a day. He urged as his only apology that he had first taken it to assuage an intolerable gnawing pain of hunger in his stomach and in time he became a chronic addict. As late as 1848, he went for sixty-one days without any opium at all, but it was reported that his writing abilities decreased following days of abstinence. (*Sheffield Times*)

MARCH 8TH

1862: Today it was announced that the Mayor, John Browns Esq., 'has caused a very beautiful memorial window to be placed in the chancel of the Sheffield parish church in honour of his parents. The subject of the stained-glass window is the "History of Joseph" and it represents five events in the life of Joseph. They are Joseph sold to the Ishmaelites, Joseph in prison, Joseph before Pharaoh, Joseph riding in the chariot, and Joseph made known to his brethren'. The reporter describes that: 'in one compartment there are angels supporting a scroll which is inscribed with the Fifth Commandment. The tracery also has beautiful angels bearing scrolls with different inscriptions drawn on them. The execution of the window is in the highest style of art and does give great credit to Mr Drury (to whom Mr Brown gave the order) and to Messrs Baillie of London, the stained glass experts. It will be remembered that these gentlemen produced that superb subject in glass in the 1851 Exhibition entitled "Shakespeare reading his play to Queen Elizabeth", which was widely acclaimed. The cost of this memorial window was in the region of £160 and it was said to be a great asset to the church'. (*Sheffield Daily Telegraph*)

MARCH 9TH

1892: The long-awaited performance of the singer Nikita took place at the Albert Hall. Large crowds flocked to come and hear the singer, who was also known to many as 'the American Nightingale'. Nikita has been giving concerts in most of the towns in the Yorkshire area and her fame had been increasing. She performed on March 9th with other first-class musicians in what was to be the last, grand concert of the season in Sheffield. Nikita aroused great acclaim and enthusiasm everywhere she went, so her arrival was awaited with great impatience. She had a standing ovation when she took to the stage at the Albert Hall. Each song was met with cries of 'encore', with people standing and cheering. She also sang songs in German and Russian, as well as English, leaving her audience spellbound. At the conclusion of the last song, she was met with such enthusiastic applause that she reappeared no less than nine times, before the concert could proceed again. It was noted that the audience consisted of many of the most well-known families of the town and was a significant event in Sheffield's history. (*Sheffield Star*)

MARCH 10TH

1843: It was reported on this day that a prisoner named William Furniss, who had been waiting to be sent for his trial at the assizes, absconded from the prison cells in Sheffield. This impudent prisoner left the cells carrying away with him the gaoler's watch. There were seven prisoners in custody on the Tuesday and they were all in the yard together in the evening. Five of the prisoners, including Furniss, were put into a cell for the night. Whilst Constable Cooper was attending to two other prisoners, Furniss managed to slip out of the not yet locked cell and hide in a side yard. Cooper locked the cell door without counting the prisoners. He then retired to bed at midnight, and, on awaking at 2.30 a.m., he found the window open and that a door leading out of the bedroom into an outer passage was also open. His watch, to the value of £8, which had been laid on a table at the side of his bed, had been stolen. He later found that the thief had even taken some of his tobacco from a box that lay on the table. Handbills were published and Furniss was re-taken at Nottingham later the same afternoon. (*Sheffield Iris*)

MARCH 11TH

1864: The Dale Dyke Dam (built in 1853) burst and was the cause of one of the worst disasters in Sheffield's history. It was estimated after the disaster that almost 250 people had been killed and approximately 4,000 houses were damaged. It was nearly midnight and the lanterns of the engineers inspecting the dam bobbed up and down could still be seen on the embankment. The resident Engineer was working right under the part of the dam where the waves were lapping against the edge. He was called to safety by a distressed shout, and several minutes later the centre of the embankment collapsed, releasing 114 million cubic feet of water, which thundered down the valley. It struck the sleeping village of Malin Bridge and surged up the Rivelin Valley and across the level meadows of Hillsborough. From Brightside to Low Bradfield stretched a broad ribbon of destruction. In the frothing water, corpses of men, women and children, animals, half-dead things still struggling, trees, furniture, machinery and stones swirled and drifted. The water destroyed nearly every bridge it passed through until it got to Lady Bridge in Sheffield. At Neepsend, acres of houses were made derelict and whole families were swept away. (Walton, M., *Sheffield: Its Story and its Achievements*, Sheffield, Amethyst Press, 1984)

MARCH 12TH

1859: On this day, it was reported that the state of trade in Sheffield was much improved over the previous few months. The reporter states with great pride that: 'We hear of several of our firms being moderately busy, and though by no means fully engaged, they have no reason to complain, when business of the town generally is known to be much below the average. If therefore there should be any improvement it must be understood to be very partial. We cannot help thinking there is every probability that an impetus will be given to our staple branches when the feelings of uncertainty lately engendered is in a moderate degree removed. In this opinion our continental houses will no doubt concur. It will be noticed that Mr Allen proposes to cover internal copper wiring of electric cables with twisted steel wire. We also see that Mr James Spurr has patented a process for making tin plate of steel instead of iron and we understand that the internal part of the Armstrong gun is to be made of steel'. It was hoped that these new innovations and opportunities would open out a new branch of trade for what may have then been called Sheffield's native commodity of iron and steel manufacture. (*Sheffield Times*)

MARCH 13TH

1864: A report was published in the *Sheffield Independent* on an exhibition of Mr Soyers Magic Stove at the Cutler's Hall under the eye of the 'gastronomic regenerator' himself, which was held on March 12th. Two or three of the 'magic stoves' were in operation and were cooking omelettes, cutlets and so on before the eyes of the audience. The stove was described as 'a species of copper with a furnace opening and a flue passing from this opening, near the bottom of one of its sides through the middle and up the centre to the top'. On this was placed a frying pan or stew pan, saucepan, kettle or coffee pot. The whole contraption stood upon a tray about 14in long and was certainly clean in its operation. It was anticipated that a gentleman may cook his steak or his chop on his study table, or a lady may have it among her crochet and other works. It was also an indispensable appendage to the breakfast table. The stove could well be an advantage to the traveller's equipment or be part of the paraphernalia of a picnic. It was reported that Mr Soyer had donated one of his stoves to the Mayoress as a gesture of thanks for his invitation to Sheffield. (*Sheffield Independent*)

MARCH 14TH

1856: An account of the 'Sheffield' display at Crystal Palace in London appeared in the *Sheffield Courant* in which the reporter stated that, since his last visit, the Sheffield Court had greatly augmented its attractions. He continued that, 'many of our manufacturers have sent to the Crystal Palace splendid specimens of Sheffield workmanship. They have very ingeniously resolved to make the Sheffield Court itself a place of protracted sojourn, by many of those persons who have wearied themselves by their rambles among the wonders of Sydenham'. They accomplished this by placing in the midst of the Court a magnificent ottoman of octagonal form covered with dark crimson velvet and offering luxurious sitting accommodation to more than twenty persons. On March 14th, when the reporter visited, there were hundreds of people looking at the exhibits and vying for a place on the ottoman. The ottoman was surmounted by a figure bearing two banners, one displaying the coat of arms of the City of Sheffield and the other the Cutler's Company. Around its centre was a variety of specimens of cutlery and silver under plate glass. This ottoman had been specially manufactured for the exhibition by Messrs George Eadon & Sons of Sheffield. (*Sheffield Courant*)

MARCH 15TH

1854: A letter from Paris was printed in the French newspaper *Galignani* today, asking for subscriptions from British people in France for the sufferers of the Sheffield flood as a result of the Dale Dyke dam having burst its banks. The letter writer, who signed himself Evocatus Paratus, writes: 'Our hearts are all moved by the recital of the dread calamity that has just desolated a fair, populous and thriving district of our dear England. Assuredly, the first emotion of every English heart will be to wish to do what may be done to succour those who have suddenly been reduced from comfort and prosperity to distress and poverty. Let those who live in this city make no delay but by a ready, active and practical sympathy, testify that the English in Paris feel a deep and lively interest in the sorrows, as in the joy of their native land.' It seems that at the same time requests for subscription for the victims of the flood were made by English clergymen, as well as ministers from the pulpits of Paris. Collections were also being made in the Parisian streets, such was the pitiable state of the people of Sheffield. The proprietor of the paper promised to send all subscriptions to the proper quarter. (*Sheffield Courant*)

MARCH 16TH

1848: James Morton (22) was brought before the York Assizes charged with Sacrilege. He was charged that on the evening of December 10th 1847, he broke into the Church of St Mary's in Sheffield and stole thirteen gas brackets. The sexton, James Dyson, told the court that in the morning he had found a broken window, which had been used by a thief to gain entrance into the church. The church plate had been locked away and the only things that had been stolen were the brackets. A few days after the robbery, Morton offered the brackets to an associate named Luke Bishop of Pea Croft, saying that they belonged to a man who was waiting outside on the street. Bishop was suspicious and asked him to bring the man in from the street, but the prisoner went out and did not return until the following day. The brackets were placed into the custody of PC Silk and were then identified by the sexton. The prisoner went on the run and was not apprehended until February 4th 1848. After a very short trial, he was found guilty and sentenced to imprisonment with hard labour for nine months. (*Sheffield Independent*)

March 17th

1874: At about 2.30 a.m., it was reported that there was a large fire on Kelham Island in the premises of Messrs Wheatman and Smith, saw manufacturers of the Russell Works. The seat of the fire had been in the 'hardening room' of the saw department. In this room there were several large vats of oil, one of which contained upwards of 250 gallons. For reasons unknown, these were ignited, and within minutes the room became an inferno. The fire brigade was summoned, but their efforts to save anything in the room proved futile. In fact, the water from the hosepipes seemed to increase the flames the firemen then wisely directed their efforts to prevent the spread of the flames to the surrounding buildings on either side. A group of offices and a flax mill were saved thanks to the quick thinking of the fire officer, Captain James Booth. At the time the *Sheffield Independent* reporter left the scene, it was supposed that the fire would in all probability burn for quite a few hours before being extinguished completely. (*Sheffield Independent*)

MARCH 18TH

1879: On this day in Parliament, it was announced that William Habron, who had been convicted at York Assizes of the murder of PC Cock, would be granted a free pardon. Mr Cross, the local MP for Sheffield, had requested an inquiry into the matter, after Charlie Peace admitted to the murder of PC Cock whilst burgling a house at Whalley Range. He announced to the House that he met with law officers of the Crown Court, and the assize judge who had tried the case in August of 1876. They agreed that the Peace's confession completely exonerated Habron. He stated that, 'It might be a source of satisfaction to the House, as it was to himself, to know that he did so with the full concurrence of the learned judge. It had never been the practice in this country to give compensation, but he might be allowed to state that he saw his way to making such arrangements under which care, that in the future this unfortunate and unhappy man should be attended to.' Mr M. Henry MP gave notice that on Monday he would ask what steps the Rt Hon gentleman intended to take in order to compensate Habron. (*Birmingham Daily Post*)

MARCH 19TH

1831: The *Sheffield Independent* ran an advert on this day for Messrs Fryer and Wilcock, who offered lessons in arithmetic to tradespeople of the town. The reporter stated that, 'we had not the least doubt of their success on inspecting their testimonial book, which contains some hundreds of testimonials. But at the same time were of the opinion that the majority of the public who were not acquainted with the flattering nature of the testimonials, remained cautious until they had the opinion of some of their own town's people'. The book contained many comments from individuals well known in the town. Amongst them, the reporter noted, were three testimonials from the principals of the first Ladies Seminaries in Sheffield. One such read: 'we the undersigned highly approve of the system of calculating as taught by Mr Fryer and recommended the same to those who have a desire for improvement, conceiving it will answer their highest expectations, both in commercial and domestic affairs'. The terms of Messrs Fryers and Wilcock's tuition fees were very modest. For six lessons lasting two hours each, the tutors would charge a guinea, for two or three students studying together the cost was 16*s*, and for six students they would each be charged 11*s*. (*Sheffield Independent*)

MARCH 20TH

1858: A solar eclipse took place on this day. A reporter noted that: 'the sky had begun to get thick and cloudy about 11.45 a.m. and by noon the edge of the moon was seen to be gradually stealing over the sun, which could clearly be seen with the naked eye. At times, however, the sun was so powerful that one had to wear coloured glasses. The effect at this moment was beautiful. The gradual changing of the sun's crescent form was clearly seen; and as the atmosphere became darker a kind of purple shadow appeared to envelope everyone. It was so dark that in houses the residents could barely see to read. This lasted for 3 minutes and 40 seconds'. The reporter continued that: 'By the aid of a telescope, we could clearly distinguish the spots on the sun, particularly a large and uneven spot near the centre. At the commencement of the eclipse the thermometer stood at 44.3 degrees Fahrenheit but gradually fell to 41.7 degrees. This explains that, although a large quantity of light was given by such a small proportion of the sun's disc, the heat did not travel in the same proportion.' (*Sheffield Times*)

MARCH 21ST

1864: An account was printed in the *Sheffield Courant* detailing the lucky escape of a family from the Sheffield flood. John Parkes of Orchard Street told a reporter that he and his family were awakened by the cry 'escape to the tip' – this being the name given to the railway embankment which stands close to the house that he and his family occupied. The cry was instantly followed by 'Fire! Fire!' Thinking that either his house was on fire, or that a tremendous fire raged in the neighbourhood, both he and his wife seized one of their children and rushed downstairs. Before he could open the door, water burst in, throwing him, his wife and his two children back with incredible force. He felt himself whirling around in the flood and heard his wife cry out, but remembers no more. Those who saw him later stated that he was about to be washed out of one of the windows when he grabbed a shutter and, pulling himself from there, managed to get onto the roof, where he was later rescued. His wife and both children were drowned and their bodies later identified by him at the Sheffield workhouse, where most of the 250 bodies of victims of the flood had been taken. (*Sheffield Courant*)

MARCH 22ND

1871: On this day, a number of papers carried the report of a Sheffield man who had died whilst incarcerated in Wakefield House of Correction. An inquest had been held on the previous day on a man named James Speight, a file cutter, who had been sentenced on November 26th last for stealing money at Sheffield. The man was eighteen years of age when he was admitted to the prison the following day. The prison surgeon, Dr Wood, told the coroner, Mr T. Taylor, that when he had been admitted to the prison he was very thin and emaciated and claimed to have a tic. He was employed at sorting fibres until January 12th, when he complained of diarrhoea and was sent into the hospital. In a day or two, typhoid fever developed, but after a short time he appeared to have recovered, albeit still having some bouts of diarrhoea. On Sunday, he complained of great pain and died that same evening when the doctor was in attendance. He had been due to be discharged on February 24th, but, as Dr Wood certified that he was still very poorly, he agreed to remain in the prison hospital. The jury returned a verdict of death from natural causes. (*Yorkshire Post*)

MARCH 23RD

1846: This evening, the town of Sheffield was delighted by an art exhibition in the Mechanics Institute. It was reported that the exhibits 'have been displayed to perfection by Mr J.G. Wightman and Mr Edwin Smith'. The show included the sculpture of a lion, which had been made for the Duke of Norfolk by Mr E. Smith. There was also a cast of a colossal statue of Aristides, and in each of the four corners of the saloon stood four beautiful figures. Several pictures were lent to the exhibition, four of which were from the Master Cutler from the Cutler's Hall. Glass cases were arranged along the walls and in the centre of the room, which were furnished with rare contributions to the exhibition. There were many specimens of Dresden china from Derby, alongside exquisite papier mâché goods from Birmingham. The far side of the saloon had a large, atmospheric railway and the near side held the refreshment stall. The vestibule and staircase were replete with works of art and curiosities. It was hoped that the event would not just be a sop to the curious, but that it would also provide a means of cultivating public taste to promote popular education. (*Sheffield Independent*)

March 24th

1871: On this day, Dame schools were criticised by the Sheffield School Board as not supplying sufficient education to children. A report stated that at the thirty-three Dame schools in the town, the instructions given were altogether insufficient for children over five years of age. Indeed, the conclusion as to whether the instruction of children of any age ought to be entrusted to any of the teachers in charge of these schools was doubtful. The majority of teaching staff was female, many of them being elderly or widows, who were earning a scanty livelihood rather than choosing to be dependent on the parish. The education of a large majority of them was very limited; some of them were even unable to spell simple words of two syllables correctly. The rooms where the children were taught were far too small, and the curriculum was said to only include reading classes. The presence of text books was non-existent, and, in addition to this, many attended to household work whilst teaching. Children paid 1*d* or 2*d* for their tuition, yet a large number of them aged between ten and twelve were not able to write their own names. In one of the houses, pupils were taught in a small room which contained a male teacher's bed, which the children were forced to use as a seat. (Walton, M., *Sheffield: Its Story and its Achievements*, Wakefield, Amethyst Press, 1984)

MARCH 25TH

1872: An inquest was held at the Wellington Inn, Langsett Road, Walkley on the death of Mary Emma Sergeant; a single aged thirty-five who had committed suicide the previous day. Her father, a farmer living on Creswick Street, Walkley, stated that his daughter had returned from service due to ill health eleven months previously. She remained ill, complaining that she got very little sleep as she could see imaginary figures in her bedroom. On Friday morning he was just about to rise when he heard her cry out, 'Oh father I am dying'. He went into her bedroom and told her that she didn't look as if she was dying, but she showed him a packet of Battle's Vermin Killer, saying the she had taken some. A doctor, Mr Packman, was summoned and immediately proceeded to give her a stomach pump, but it was too late and she died in her father's arms. The coroner told the jury that there was clear evidence that she had taken her own life and it was their duty to decide what state of mind she was in at the time. The jury returned a verdict of 'suicide whilst temporarily insane'. (*Sheffield Times*)

MARCH 26TH

1844: A case of arson was reported today in the *Sheffield Mercury*. Responsible for the sudden rise in cases were a group that later became known as the Luddites. The reported stated, somewhat sadly, that: 'We are sorry to record another attempt at this diabolical crime. The machinery in the wheel at the Wharncliffe side, near Oughtbridge, was set on fire on Saturday night last. The incendiaries kindled two different fires upon the premises, burning and destroying the drums and the ends of the water wheels, together with the grinders, pulleys, and the leather straps carrying the machinery; these proceeds are most outrageous and unjustifiable. It used to be deemed sufficient to carry off the wheel bands of an obnoxious grinder, but now it seems to be the fashion to destroy the property of the owner of the wheel. This is the second time this scandalous transaction has occurred in the short space of six months'. (*Sheffield Merury*)

MARCH 27TH

1821: The premises of Mr S. Turner of the Barrack Tavern were burgled and 50s in copper was taken. It was supposed that the thief, who climbed in through a back window, was acting alone and must have been well acquainted with the premises – knowing exactly where it was possible to break in. After breaking into the pub, he went to the cellar, where Mr Turner was in the habit of keeping his keys. Opening the bar door, he rewarded himself with eggs, beefsteak and tea, and then left the property with the copper, making sure that none of the inmates of the house, who slept in the attic, were disturbed. It seems that the thief was satisfied with his booty, as there was a large quantity of wearing apparel, several hams and liquor left in the tavern. It was thought he was certainly an audacious thief, but, arguably, he could not have been deemed a greedy one. Mr Turner had a pretty good idea of the person whom he suspected for this *friendly* visit, but at the time, he did not have sufficient proof to warrant his apprehension. However, he gave full details of the suspect in question to the police. (*Sheffield Independent*)

MARCH 28TH

1840: John Walker (25) was indicted at the Sheffield Magistrates Court for stealing money belonging to George Chapman, George Dobson and Nathan Longley. The prisoner pleaded guilty to the charge. The persons from whom the money was stolen were the children of the above men, who had been sent to collect the wages on the Saturday evening from their employers. The prisoner had met the children in the street on three separate occasions and, by some pretext or other, he had gained their confidence and taken the money from them. The court was told that Walker had been convicted of similar felonies three times previously, also involving children. The jury took little time to find Walker guilty. The magistrate, in passing sentence, said a realisation came to him in the duration of the trial – he had 'never met with a man who had resorted to such disgraceful means as the prisoner had made use of'. He told Walker that he was giving him a severe punishment in the hope that the people of Sheffield would be safe from his crimes for some while and he then sentenced him to be transported for seven years. (*Sheffield Independent*)

MARCH 29TH

1850: A number of vendors selling unwholesome meat at Sheffield were reported by members of the public. A random examination was made by health inspectors, who found five butchers in possession of seven calves of a character 'so clearly unfit for human food' that the vendors had no option but to give them up to the inspectors to destroy. The guilty shopkeepers were taken to the Town Hall, where they were charged with the sale of spoiled meat. The public were made aware that gone-off meat had been found in the possession of a large number of vendors, but they were unaware that the process by which they found it was through random inspection. The *Sheffield Independent* reporter stated, 'we have the reassurance of the police that all the butchers will be prosecuted and fined. The names of those butchers guilty of selling such meat were not given to this reporter but the public will be made aware when the cases come to court, and their names can at last be revealed.' He further states that, 'this paper begs that meat inspectors have a more thorough and careful way of inspections, done on a regular and ad hoc basis to determine that these purveyors of unwholesome meat are eradicated from our town'. (*Sheffield Independent*)

MARCH 30TH

1850: A coroner's jury was shocked to hear of the murder of a newly born baby by its mother. A young girl called Maria Woodall was suspected of being pregnant by her mother and her sister, which she categorically denied. Meanwhile, her sister got married and went to live in Bright Street, and Maria was invited to stay. On the Sunday morning, she told her sister that she felt unwell and went to lie down on the bed. At about 4 p.m., her sister found her in 'a great state' and called the surgeon, Mr James Gregory, who told her that Maria had given birth and demanded to know where the baby was. At first, Maria tried to deny it, but after searching the room, the body of a newborn baby girl was found. It was reported that 'around its neck was a cord so tight that it was impossible to put a finger through' and a constable was called. Weeping so much that her sister thought that she was insane, Maria finally admitted to killing the child. She was taken before the magistrate, who found her guilty, and she was ordered to take her trial at the next assizes. (*Yorkshire Post*)

MARCH 31ST

1850: An enquiry had been made on the churchyard of St Peters parish church of Sheffield. On this day, a report appeared which stated that St Peters was one of the oldest burial places in Sheffield, having been used for over 600 years, and that it was estimated to hold over 10,000 graves. The report reads: 'This graveyard is surrounded by inhabited houses closely on three sides and is six feet above the level of the houses in some parts. It is frequently necessary to lade water out of the graves in the clay part of the ground. The drainage sometimes comes out into the streets and at other places it reaches the lower part of the town and exudes into the wells from which the poor are supplied with water. At times, this churchyard is very offensive and is said to affect the health of the inhabitants in the neighbourhood.' Ending the report with a recommendation that something be done about the graveyard, the report warned that, 'from the crowded state of the churchyard, practices of a very disgusting and indecent kind are resorted to by the gravediggers'. (Batty, S.R., *Sheffield*, London, Ian Allen Publishers, 1984)

APRIL 1ST

1857: An inquest was held at the Red House Inn on Solly Street on the death of a sixty-seven-year-old man named Colquhoun, who had been found dead in bed the previous morning at his house on Kenyon Street. It seems that he had been a widower for seventeen years, but for three of those years had lived with a woman named Staniforth. For the last three weeks of his life, he had been drinking heavily and continuously. On the evening prior to his death, he went to bed in a near-paralytic state. The next morning, he remained insensible and was unable to make himself understood by Staniforth when she got up at seven o'clock. On returning back to the bedroom at about eleven o'clock, she found him dead in bed. A policeman on duty in the neighbourhood was called in and he found a large amount of empty bottles, the contents of which Staniforth had just emptied. Not being satisfied with her answers, information was given to the coroner, who ordered a post-mortem. It revealed that nearly all of the organs were in a diseased state and that death had been due to a combination of this and excessive drinking. (*Sheffield Free Press*)

APRIL 2ND

1861: At the meeting of the Sheffield workhouse guardians, it was requested that they elect a new master of the workhouse. Following the death of Mr S. Rogers, advertisements for the post had been inserted in several local newspapers. The committee appointed for such matters had inspected the applications and several men had been requested to attend the board this morning for selection. The first to attend was Mr James Westoe, the master of the Boys' Charity School; John Bennet, the assistant relieving officer at Sheffield and formerly assistant master at Sudbury workhouse, and Charles Edwin Davies, schoolmaster of Whittington, Chesterfield. Another applicant was Samuel Jenkinson, a farmer from Hooton Roberts, whose application, it was remarked, had 'excited some merriment' with the Selection Committee. Other applications were from two former masters of Congleton and Bromsgrove workhouses, a schoolteacher, and a carriage builder. After some discussion, it was decided that the election would be made by secret voting. The results were: Mr Westoe – seven votes; Mr Bennett – four votes, and Mr Davies – one vote. Mr Westoe was then unanimously elected for the post with the request that his duties start as soon as possible. (*Sheffield Post*)

April 3rd

1833: An announcement was made that enquiries were being made by the Board of Trade, respecting the state of Sheffield's various manufacturers. This was intended to be for the information of the government in reference to a commercial treaty, which was being arranged on the basis of mutual concessions between England and France. For this purpose, the Master Cutler had made enquiries of several of the principles manufacturers of Sheffield. These were to include iron and steel goods, plated goods and cutlery. In the course of the negotiations, France had displayed a willing disposition to receive Sheffield goods. It was anticipated that a treaty could be negotiated on very favourable terms, due to the fact that they were less likely to interfere with the profits of their own French manufacturers. If this treaty was to be successful, then Sheffield might have reasonably calculated some vast improvements in trade. It would be remembered by many people of the town how excellent a market France had proved for Sheffield goods previous to the war. It would also be in the memory of contemporary manufacturers at a time when most Sheffield houses had resident agents in Paris as well as French agents in the area. (*Morning Post*)

APRIL 4TH

1829: This evening a dreadful occurrence took place at St George's Church, Sheffield. A little before the commencement of divine service, a man by the name of Robert Barber, residing in Broad Lane, fell down in a fit of apoplexy in the body of the church. Unfortunately, before he could be removed into the porch, he was dead. His wife, who had accompanied her husband to church, was deeply distressed and was cared for by other ladies at the service. Mr Ray, a surgeon of the city, was in the church and immediately attended upon the poor man but found that his life was extinct. The Revd S. Langstone, the minister, led the congregation in a prayer for the poor man's soul and suitably alluded to the incident in his sermon as an illustration of the Scriptures' assertion that 'in the midst of life we are in death'. The story quickly went about the town, and other clergymen used the incident in part of their sermon; including Revd T. Lessey, who noted the circumstances in a very solemn and affecting manner at the close of his sermon in Carver Street Chapel the same evening. (*Sheffield Courant*)

APRIL 5TH

1879: As a result of industrial distress, which was then rife in the town, several sewing depots had been set up for women and girls of the town. On this day, and as a result of the upturn in the industrial trades, a final meeting was held at the West Street depot. In order to thank the women for all their hard work, they were treated to tea by the Master Cutler. A presentation was made to the Ladies' Sewing Committee, headed by the Mayoress of Sheffield, by some of the women. The presentation was a small address written carefully on a white card, which stated that: 'the women employed in sewing on Tuesday and Fridays for the last few weeks, wish to give their sincere thanks to all the ladies who have given their time and attention in administering to their wants, not only temporal but spiritual too'. Several other similar addresses were given to the members of the other Sewing Committees, of which there were several. At 3 p.m., the Revd W. Milton gave a farewell address and his thanks to the women. (*Sheffield Independent*)

April 6th

1876: A 'breach of promise' case was heard today at Leeds assizes. Jane Ann Hurst, a single woman of Barnsley, prosecuted Frank Rice Greathead, a silversmith of Sheffield. The couple met on May 3rd 1873 at a wedding, where Miss Hurst was a bridesmaid. Several letters were exchanged which indicated Mr Greathead's wish to marry Miss Hurst and they considered themselves to be engaged. On March 23rd 1874, he told her that he was looking for a house for them both and agreed that they would be married the following May. A fortnight later, he went to Barnsley to inform her that the engagement was at an end. He demanded his letters back, as they would prove that he had asked her to marry him, and they agreed on a meeting place. However, instead of his letters, she gave him a parcel with pages from an almanac in and a note saying 'sold again'. Miss Hurst told the court that she had been engaged three times, once before she met Greathead and once since. The jury retired to consider how much compensation should be awarded and they agreed on £10. (*Morning Post*)

APRIL 7TH

1869: Today's newspapers reported a case brought before the court at Sheffield Town Hall of a man was charged with not having his child vaccinated for smallpox when ordered by a magistrate. The man, a grocer and beer seller of Hillfoot named James Collis, fully admitted the charge and announced his determination not to have the child vaccinated. He said his child was healthy, born of healthy parents, and he had seen two children in his neighbourhood die from being vaccinated. The magistrate told him that in ignoring an order imposed by the law, they not only had the power to fine him, but they could also prosecute him for disobedience. The prosecutor, Mr Dunn, pointed out that a fine of 20s was the law in such cases, but that didn't help the public if their safety was put into jeopardy by the child catching the disease. The defence stated that the whole compulsory Vaccination Act was under review at that moment. Mr Collis was then fined 20s and costs and Mr Dunn urged him to reconsider his way of thinking, but he remained unconvinced and said, 'he would never go against his own flesh and blood'. (*Daily Telegraph*)

APRIL 8TH

1840: On this day, an account was printed in the *Sheffield Mercury* on the rise in employment of climbing boys, or chimneysweeps. The reporter wrote: 'amongst the many evils which demand the attention of the legislators and philanthropists is that of employing *young children* to sweep chimneys. It is indeed astonishing that thinking people should tolerate such a practice and it is the more astonishing because its victims are taken from the most helpless class – *little children*. Many persons can now testify to the efficiency of the chimney sweeping machine instead of using children. In this town a person called Jepson who was demonstrating his machine let it be known that he was sweeping the chimney at a house and crowds flocked to watch it. Amongst the crowd were four sweeps who predicted its failure. Jepson had no difficulty at all. He was then challenged to sweep the chimney confessed to be a difficult one. There he did find it difficult, not from any failure of the machine but that fact that it hadn't been cleaned for many years. With a degree of patience he persevered and at last sent the brush through the pot amidst the shouts of the spectators.' (*Sheffield Mercury*)

APRIL 9TH

1833: At the Town Hall today, a case was heard about manufacturers counterfeiting another's 'mark'. Mr Verdon Brittain accused Mr William Harrison, a razor manufacturer, for striking an imitation of his mark, which had been granted for his sole use by the Corporation of Cutlers. A clause in the Cutler Company Act imposed a penalty of £20 upon any person who shall 'counterfeit or imitate' any mark granted by them to any manufacturer of cutlery. Mr Brittain called witnesses to prove that they had worked for Mr Harrison and struck the initials G & B upon his razors, two of which were produced. Mr Harrison stated that he had used the same mark openly for eight years and that it was C & B, not G. On those grounds he claimed that there was no evidence for calling it a counterfeit of Mr Brittain's mark. Mr Brittain stated that the mark was done for the purpose of deceiving people and that he had received orders from South America asking for goods marked C & B. Revd G. Chandler, the magistrate who heard the case, said he could not think it was intended as an imitation and therefore he dismissed the summons. (*Sheffield Iris*)

APRIL 10TH

1850: A letter was delivered to the offices of the *Sheffield Independent* complaining about a recent attack on the rooks in Gell Street. The letter stated that 'the public were well aware that a colony of rooks established themselves in that vicinity following the disturbance over fifty years ago when Mr Wilkinson's stacks were set on fire at Broomhall, where there was a large rookery'. The letter writer goes on to claim that a disgraceful outrage has been committed on the birds: 'these interesting and favourite birds have attracted the kindliest feeling towards them on the part of the whole neighbourhood. They have just finished filling their eggs with their now numerous nests. No hand had been raised against them until yesterday, when a ruffian decided to fire on them and killed two nesting birds. I am at a loss to execrate this act of atrocious barbarity. I sincerely hope that this individual will be identified and brought before the magistrates for shooting from a public highway'. The *Sheffield Independent* concluded that 'the laws of Moses, of common sense and of sporting instincts rightly condemn such unmanly conduct and we agree with the letter writer that the interests of justice will be preserved when this man is brought before the magistrates and charged'. (*Sheffield Independent*)

APRIL 11TH

1844: An inquest was held today on the body of a newborn female child, found in a goit by Old Park Wood. Robert Booker of Philadelphia, who worked on the railway, was on his way to work about 5.10 a.m. on Wednesday when he saw a bundle wrapped in a blue and white handkerchief in the river at Brightside Bierlow. He pulled the bundle out of the water and began to unwrap it when he saw the body of a child. A constable was called, and, with the permission of the coroner, the corpse was taken to the workhouse. An order was given to the bellman to cry out the circumstances in three parishes, but nothing was heard of the mother. A surgeon, Mr John Sykes, was called and he told the coroner that there had been no outward sign of injury and he gave his opinion that the child was five or six days old. From the state of the body, it was be almost impossible to say how the child had died. The jury recorded a verdict of death by unknown circumstances. (*Sheffield Independent*)

APRIL 12TH

1867: This evening an accident happened at the Brightside Colliery, owned by Messrs Unwin and Shaw, resulting in the loss of five colliers. The five men, who were all married, were named as Thomas Bates, James and George Fox, John Gouldstraw and Joseph Burgin. The colliery was one that worked both a day and a night shift and the deceased men were working the night shift from 8 p.m. to 4 a.m. They got into the cage. which lowered them down into the workings. The cages were made of strong metal, with iron bars to hold the men inside. They operated along with another cage, which lifted up the coal from the mine. The cage holding the men had only gone a few yards when the cable snapped, sending the cage 200 yards to the bottom. The man operating the lift only realised what had happened when he heard the men scream and he saw the broken cable. Rescuers entering by a 'drift way' found the cage broken into a thousand pieces and the other cage used to pull up coal was also smashed to pieces. The bodies of the unfortunate men were mangled beyond description. (*Daily Telegraph*)

APRIL 13TH

1863: On this day, Henry Light and Edward Hides stood trial in York on charges of forging 'greenbacks', which were paper currency issued during the American Civil War. Several months previously it became known to the police and the American authorities that an engraver in Sheffield was reported as doing 'a brisk trade' in forging these notes. A famous London detective, Sergeant Spital, was sent to Sheffield to work with the Sheffield police and an American Vice Consul to arrest these forgers. A reward for information was offered and this resulted in a letter which included a name and address, giving the name of the forger as Light and one of his workmen as Hides. These two men had forged large numbers of notes, from $5 to $10. The men were finally arrested and brought in front of the magistrates where they were sentenced to stand trial at the York Assizes. It was also reported that another two men had been arrested in Worksop who had on their person, several of these forged 'greenbacks'. At the York Assizes, Light was sentenced to four years in prison and Hides to fifteen months. (*Sheffield Independent*)

APRIL 14TH

1899: This evening, a talk was given by Dr Barnado of the Dr Barnado Homes for Orphan Waifs at the reception room at the Town Hall. Attended by the Mayor, Alderman W.E. Clegg and the Lady Mayoress, Dr Barnado told the crowd that one of the MPs for Sheffield, Sir Howard Vincent, was the vice president of the homes. He said the greatest progress made during the reign of Her Majesty was in the position of children, both in law and in public opinion. More protection to waifs and strays had been given through such organisations as the NSPCC, which could not be too highly extolled. The Barnado Homes had received a total of 966 children from Sheffield and other Yorkshire areas between the years 1892 and 1898, and many had not any idea of the most basic elements of religion at all. These children were now starting lives of industry and hope, instead of begging and thievery. At the end of his talk, a collection was taken which realied £38. Thanks were extended by the Mayor to Dr Barnado and he was invited to take tea with them in an adjoining room. (*Sunday Telegraph*)

APRIL 15TH

1899: The body of a young whale, which had been captured in the River Trent, could be seen on this day in the yard of the Green Dragon at Attercliffe. The whale had been spotted near the mouth of the River Idle, close to West Stockwith, a few days previously. Crowds of people had been attracted to see the whale, amongst whom were many women and children. The whale was reported to be 14ft long, and 3ft 5in broad at the tail, and weighing nearly a ton. The whale had been captured by Sam Farr and seven other young boatmen on March 27th. Farr saw the whale sporting about in the centre of the river and twice it came near to the side of their boat, but not near enough to reach it. When it came near a third time, they succeeded in sticking a boat hook into the left side of its jaw and drew it onto the bank, where they tied it to a hedge. It was something like 48 hours before the whale expired. Since that time, Farr and his companions exhibited the whale, which was the largest known to have been caught inland. *(Yorkshire Post)*

APRIL 16TH

1951: On this day, Winston Churchill was given the Freedom of the City of Sheffield. In the evening, a crowd of 3,000 people at the City Hall watched him sign the illuminated scroll. Mr Churchill said that in 1943, the Sheffield City Council unanimously decided with a Socialist majority to offer him the freedom, and this he valued highly. Although his political opponents on the council far outnumbered the other members, it was again a unanimous decision which had brought him to Sheffield. Such actions carried a message to foreign countries, who might not understand when they read of Britain's fierce party contentions that underneath there was a deep unity. He paid tribute to Mr Bevin, who had recently died, aand whom he described as a great friend and countryman. Churchill stated that: 'he was a man who demonstrated with an unchallengeable right the characteristics of trade unions, and also the virtues of our race of which we are justly proud. Mr Bevin showed how it was possible to make your way in this free democracy of ours, from the humblest situation to the greatest and the most responsible employments in the State'. (*The Times*)

APRIL 17TH

1854: Yet another house was blown up by a home-made bomb in the trade union disputes which ravaged Sheffield during these years. This particular incident happened at some very secluded houses on Abbeydale Road, Millhouses, about three miles from Sheffield. The occupier was a man named Fisher, a scythe-maker, who had been a member of a trade union four years previously, but had not paid any subscriptions since that time. He had recently been told that he was 'wanted' for the unpaid subscriptions. At 1 a.m. on April 16th, he and his wife awoke to the sound of glass breaking. He looked out of the window but saw nothing until there was an explosion which lit up the room. The couple went into the adjoining room, where his apprentice usually slept, but who had fortunately gone home that night. The curtains and the window frame were ablaze, but it was quickly extinguished. It is thought the house was saved by being of old build with very thick walls. The bomb was described as a breakfast tin, filled with gunpowder and attached to a lit fuse, which was slung through a pane of glass directly into an upstairs room. (*Sheffield Examiner*)

April 18th

1838: Moses Roper, born a slave in North Carolina, spoke about his experiences at the chapel on Howard Street in front of a packed audience. He outlined from his own experience what slavery was and told the story of his escape. Moses was unusually tall (about 6ft 6in) and was described as stocky. He began by apologising for his lack of education, since it was considered a penal offence in the slave states of America to give a slave any literate instruction. He began learning English whilst in England, and he spoke it fairly well – although slowing and hesitating every so often. His narrative was highly interesting, though his manner of relating was somewhat confused. He had written a book of his experiences, which it was hoped would be sold in such numbers that every person in Sheffield would have an opportunity of reading it. In his address, Moses later exhibited a specimen of whip used regularly in slave states; to the extent that it was the habitual companion of the overseers who were known by their carrying it. It was called 'the negro flapper'. The Revd Mr Bayley then addressed the audience and the evening closed with a prayer. (*Sheffield Independent*)

APRIL 19TH

1856: A report was given in the *Sheffield Independent* on the Wicker Adult Evening Classes. At the beginning of the previous winter, several gentlemen in connection with Wicker Congregational Church opened evening classes for adults in the schoolroom in Andrew Street, where they were taught reading, writing, mental arithmetic and grammar. The group of gentlemen found the proposal so well responded to that about seventy men and youths signed up for the classes and they had an average attendance of nearly forty people. The pupils displayed such a strong desire to learn, and, aided by judicious and zealous services of the teachers, made very satisfactory improvements. As the lengthened days rendered it desirable to suspend the classes for the summer months, the sessions were brought to a close on Thursday evening. The pupils were congratulated on their excellent results as well as their steady application and they were invited to renew their attendance when the classes re-open next autumn. Some of the young men spoke in warm acknowledgement of their gratitude to their kind instructors, to whom they passed a very hearty vote of thanks. In conclusion, Revd S. Biggin commended those assembled to the Divine protection of Almighty God. (*Sheffield Independent*)

APRIL 20TH

1871: Susan Wainwright (3), the daughter of Joseph Wainwright – a pointsman on the Manchester, Sheffield and Lincolnshire Railway – met her death today after drowning in a wash tub. Her mother, who had been washing some clothes, went into the back yard to hang them on the line. Susan had been playing in the yard with the family dog and then went into the house. When her mother returned a few minutes later, she was horrified to find the child with her head in the wash tub. She immediately called in the assistance of surgeon Dr Thomas, who happened to be in the neighbourhood. Although Dr Thomas did all he could to restore consciousness, his efforts proved to be in vain. It is supposed the child fell into the tub whilst she was playing in the water. An inquest was arranged for the morning of April 21st, where it was expected that a verdict of accidental death would be returned. (*Sheffield Times*)

APRIL 21ST

1848: It was announced today that a penny news room had been opened in the town. The reporter for the *Sheffield Iris* wrote that: 'we are glad to learn that the cheap news room, recently opened by Mr Rogers, stationers at the Fruit Market, had been well patronized over the past week. For as little as 1d a day or 1s a week, patrons can read *The Times*, *Daily News*, *Sun*, *Punch* and all the Sheffield newspapers This is a good sign and very encouraging. Would the working classes become more extensive readers of the daily and weekly newspapers, they would soon understand their own rights and duties better and would be less likely to be made the dupes of the designing or the fanatic. Previous attempts to form cheap news rooms in Sheffield have been partial failures. As Mr Rogers' plan and charges are similar to what have long succeeded in Edinburgh and one or two other towns and cities, we hope this attempt will be permanently successful. It will be seen in our advertising column that Mr C.W. Cooper of South Street has also announced the opening of a news room for that district, providing he can get enough subscriptions.' (*Sheffield Iris*)

APRIL 22ND

1863: A chaotic meeting had been held on the evening of April 21st at the Temperance Hall, Town Head Street, to consider the Bill now before Parliament for closing public houses on Sunday. The meeting, which was reported in today's newspapers, was called by the Mayor (John Brown Esq.) in compliance with a most respectable signed petition bearing 1,045 signatures. The hall was crowded to excess and many were disallowed admission. The Bill introduced into the House of Commons asked that the sale of liquor be banned from 11 p.m. on Saturday night to 6 a.m. on Monday morning. Revd Canon Sale stated that he had no objection to the working man slaking his thirst after work, but he was appalled by the idea of men sitting and boozing all day on Sunday. Mr Burns declared his willingness for all pubs and clubs in the kingdom to close on Sundays. Mr John Unwin seconded the resolution, stating that he was teetotal, but they were not there to debate teetotalism but a question of great social, civil and religious importance. The meeting threatened to resort into chaos; however, when a show of hands was requested it proved that the majority were very much against Sunday closing. (*Sheffield Times*)

APRIL 23RD

1874: An account of a cruel nurse who had mistreated a child in her care was printed. A six-month-old girl, daughter of Mrs Nettleton of Milton Lane, was taken to the hospital today, suffering from injuries to her head and face. The doctor who treated her was shocked; he claimed he had not seen such injuries on a child so young before, and he immediately alerted the police constable. The constable went to interview the child's mother to establish how these injuries could have been inflicted on the little girl. It seems that she had earlier in the day been left in the care of a nurse named Eliza Ann Clarke, who, as part of her duties, carried the child to a house in Davies Street. When the child became restless, she began silencing it by cruel means. She beat the child on her head and face, blacking its eyes and inflicting other serious injuries. The constable next went to interview the nurse, but he discovered that she was only nine years old. The girl was not apprehended or prosecuted due to her age. (*Sheffield Post*)

APRIL 24TH

1831: On this day, the bodies of two highway robbers of Sheffield were put on show in the town. On the previous day, Charles Turner and James Twibell (both 19) were executed at York following their sentence at the last assizes for robbing and barbarously maltreating Jonathon Habershon on October 5th 1830. The crime took place on the King's Highway between Sheffield and Intake. There was a third robber named Priestly, who turned King's Evidence and was discharged. When the sentence of death had been passed on them, Turner wept bitterly and Twibell cried out, 'Oh Lord, spare our lives!' The bodies of two men were cut down and given to their friends for interment. It was for this purpose that the two bodies were brought to the houses of their respective friends in this neighbourhood. The newspaper stated that, 'we regret to say that news has reached us today that the "friends" of these unhappy youths have made a public exhibition of their bodies. We have also been told that the price of admission to the room where the bodies are exhibited varies according to the means of the applicant'. (Vickers, J.E., *The Unseen, the Unsightly and the Amusing*, 1997)

APRIL 25TH

1899: An account was published today of the visit of Mr Goschen, the First Lord of the Admiralty, to the annual Press Club dinner. A large portion of his speech was taken up with the justification of naval expenditure, for which he had been strongly criticised by some of his critics. He told the Press Club that it was important to maintain a fleet of naval warships as 'there is no doubt that Britain, probably out of all our continental neighbours, is the most anxious for peace. No nation wants to go to war, but if Great Britain were weak and helpless and could be easily and cheaply plundered it would be asking for trouble. Whereas, if we have a strong navy, it is simply for defensive purposes.' Mr Goschen stated that it was because of this that it was essential to keep up the navy's present strength in proportion of other powers. He told them that ninety-nine Englishmen out of every hundred would keenly oppose any diminution of the navy, which would threaten national safety. He received applause when he said that they would see that Britain's navy was adequate to the duties it might be called upon to perform. (*Sheffield Star*)

APRIL 26TH

1833: An inquest was held today after a fight between two men in a field at Low Shiregreen resulted in a death. The week before, the two men – Edward Bower and Charles Jackson – had been drinking and Bower challenged Jackson to a fight the next day. Both agreed, and, after lunch, the battle began. Edward Bower had been a prize fighter in his youth and so the fight was expected to be a tough one. After thirty or forty rounds, Jackson fell upon Bower with great force and Bower slumped to the ground quite insensible. A surgeon was called to the scene, but Bower died a few hours later. Two surgeons told the coroner that the post-mortem showed that Bower had died following a severe blow to the left side of his head. Several witnesses gave their testimony to the jury that Bower was a man who had always lived life to the full and enjoyed both food and drink. The coroner, flying against the evidence of the surgeon, summed up for the jury – declaring that he thought that Bower's death was probably brought on by apoplexy and the verdict was accidental death. (*Sheffield Courant*)

APRIL 27TH

1863: Today, a fatal accident at Chapeltown was reported in the local newspaper. It seems that on Thursday of the previous week, between 7 p.m. and 8 p.m., some people who had been working for farmer Mr John Gibson were returning from a day in the fields setting potatoes. They were on the Chapeltown to Sheffield road when the cart they were travelling in turned over, throwing everyoneon to the road; these were Benjamin Wastnedge, who was driving the cart, and three women, Sarah Steele, Eliza Drabble, and Mary Goddard. The cart was passing through a gateway when the horse turned too closely to the near side, causing one wheel to rise upon a heap of earth. The cart was upset, and, although the driver escaped without injury, the women were all hurt. Mary Goddard was left in a serious condition with injuries to her brain, and from being crushed internally; she died on Sunday night. Eliza Drabble was bruised around the right temple and suffered from internal injuries. She was able to walk about for a few days, but was subsequently confined to her bed. Sarah Steele had bruising to the forehead and a severely strained right arm, but she recovered soon after. (*Sheffield Independent*)

APRIL 28TH

1852: On this day, a robbery was reported. A servant girl was employed by Mr Wheelhouse of Portobello Street, but had absconded from the house with a quantity of valuable property. She was employed as a domestic servant in place of a regular servant, who had been taken ill. The girl, who gave her name as Maria Dowe, had applied for the post, stating to Mrs Wheelhouse that Mrs Shepherd of the Little Angel public house on West Bar had sent her. This was later found to be untrue and Mrs Shepherd had herself been robbed by the girl. At about 7 p.m., Mr and Mrs Wheelhouse left the house, leaving the girl alone with two sick children. Soon after 8 p.m., one of the little boys, who was on the sofa in the sitting room, saw the girl come downstairs with a bundle of blankets in her arms. The girl then closed the shutters of the sitting room so that the boy would not see her leaving the house. When Mr Wheelhouse returned at 9 p.m., he found that she had stolen three £5 notes, two shawls, a bonnet and some underclothing. (*Sheffield Times*)

APRIL 29TH

1838: Today's newspaper reported on an exhibition which had been on show at the Music Hall in Sheffield for the week. The displays included an oxy-hydrogen microscope, which, when demonstrated to children, gave much gratification to the young spectators. Other exhibits included a magic lantern show, a railway steam engine, and a train of carriages, which were described as 'extremely beautiful'. But it was the liberality of the Music Hall Committee which caused much comment in the local newspaper. On the Wednesday, the exhibition, the children from the Charity School had been granted free admission. The following day, the inmates of the Sheffield Workhouse went to see the exhibits, 'where their clean, comfortable and orderly appearance was pleasing to all who beheld them'. By the kindness of two unnamed gentlemen, free refreshments were also given to the inmates from the confectioner's stall. Free admission had also been offered to the soldiers in the barracks and to inmates of both of Sheffield's hospitals, as well as those attending Sunday schools and charity schools in the town. It was hoped that by the admittance of these several groups 'the attractiveness of the exhibits may continue to be unimpaired to the last'. (*Sheffield Independent*)

APRIL 30TH

1858: This morning, two notorious brothel keepers, Mrs Lee and Mrs Murphy, were brought before the bench on charges of keeping disorderly houses. The first case heard was that of Mrs Lee, whose husband was said to have a respectable job in a large firm in the town. The police gave evidence that between 1 p.m. and 2 p.m. they were called to a row at Mrs Lee's house. An officer found nine 'gentlemen' and four 'ladies', who were all clearly under the influence of alcohol. Mrs Lee said that the nine men had come to the house and demanded admittance, but as the ladies were about to retire they were refused. The men forced their way in and a melee ensued, and Mrs Lee was forced to alert the police. Mrs Murphy then appeared 'arrayed in very smart toggery, with her face as demure as possible'. Earlier that morning, at 2.45 a.m., the police had been called out and found several men and two prostitutes at the house. Mrs Murphy stated that the men came to her house drunk and she had sent for a constable to remove them. After being seriously reprimanded by the magistrates, both women were fined 10s and costs. (*Sheffield Telegraph*)

MAY 1ST

1856: At a sitting of the committee appointed to investigate the adulteration of food in Sheffield, townsman Dr Bingley was examined at some length. He declared that he was an analytical chemist and professor of chemistry at the Sheffield Medical School. He said that he believed that a corruption of goods existed among the shopkeepers and chemists of Sheffield, but that the situation had improved somewhat recently. Dr Bingley stated that among the lower class of druggists in the town he had found adulterated butter, and chicory that was mixed with peat dust. Within the past six months, he had found three cases of lime juice adulterated with pyroligneous acid. Unless lime juice was pure and contained large amounts of citric acid it was ineffectual. If a ship's crew suffered from an attack of scurvy and adulterated lime juice was administered to them, the consequences could be very bad indeed. He had found instances of food adulterated with rye, bran, potatoes and other articles. He warned that he would continue with his investigations to prevent adulteration spreading. (*Sheffield Times*)

MAY 2ND

1867: A report on the building of the new railway station for the Manchester, Sheffield and Lincolnshire Railway, which brought the new line from Chesterfield to Sheffield, was published on this day. The rapidly advancing railway made the necessity of a new station to be built, to be bounded on the east by Granville Street, on the west by Pond Lane, on the north by Harmer Lane and on the south by Turner Street. The report stated that 'one enterprising publican had re-named his house as the New Railway Hotel, but he has been forced to take his taps and barrels elsewhere as the site of his house will be swallowed up by the navies, who were to be his potential customers'. The approaches to the station were to be at the upper end of the old Haymarket. The whole distance of the River Sheaf, between Harmer Lane and Turner Street, would be spanned by three arches, which were then nearly completed. The Porter brook would be spanned by two arches, which were in a forward state, and a portion of the Bamforth dam was to be filled in. (*Daily Telegraph*)

MAY 3RD

1861: The first of two gun batches, promised by the War Office, was sent for the use of the Sheffield Artillery Corps. The members of the Corps assembled on special parade, for the purpose of escorting the guns from the station to the headquarters in Tudor Street. The Engineer Corps and the Hallamshire Rifles evinced their good feeling by joining in with the parade and the officers of the 48th Battalion sent their excellent band. The men formed themselves into parades of four apiece and marched through the streets to the station, under the command of Captain N. Creswick. The two guns, which were 32 pounders, weighing 48 cwt, had been duly mounted on two of Messrs Pickfords drays. The band of the Hallamshire Rifles played the National Anthem as the guns passed them. The parade fell in after the guns and found the streets, which had been crowded before, were now doubly so. The windows on both sides of the streets were alive with faces. The crowd assembled at the headquarters of the Artillery Corps was so strong that the parade experienced difficulty in making an entrance with their new weapons. (Vickers, J.E., *Old Sheffield Town: An Historical Miscellany*, Sheffield, Hallamshire Press, 1999)

MAY 4TH

1867: On this day, the remnants of the gibbet post of Spence Broughton were found. Broughton was hung in irons on Attercliffe Common after being executed at York in April 1792. He was a highwayman who was charged with the robbery of the Sheffield and Rotherham post. After his execution, he was put into the gibbet, where his remains were left for thirty-six years. The excavated gibbet post was a solid piece of oak, painted black and 18in in circumference. The post was described as being in a good condition, even though it had been embedded in the ground for thirty-nine years. Some 4ft 6in of this post was left, and the remainder was cut off when the gibbet was taken down thirty-seven years ago. The relic was discovered by a man called Holroyd, who was excavating the cellars of some houses on Clifton Street, Attercliffe, opposite the Yellow Lion public house. The post was taken into the grounds of the Yellow Lion, and so far, hundreds of people have visited the pub to see the historic post. (*Sheffield Independent*)

MAY 5TH

1850: The *Sheffield Times* reported on the first anniversary celebration of the Young Women's School on the Wicker. Suitable addresses were delivered and the National Anthem was sung. The pupils and the teacher afterwards attended divine service at the Queen Street chapel. This school was designed solely for young ladies and upwards of fifty, very attentive and very respectable young people attended the service a. The pupils were reported to be respectfully dressed as they marched 'crocodile fashion' back to the school, where tea was then have been provided. The reporter stated that: 'the young lady pupils are instructed in bible class, reading and writing and many of them have made considerable progress, thanks to the efforts of their teacher, Mr W. Turnell. In an effort to give the young ladies their required knowledge and only on a part time salary, Mr Turnell taught on Sunday, Monday and Tuesday evening on an unpaid and voluntary basis. It is hoped that Mr Turnell will be met with the needful pecuniary assistance as soon as possible, in order that this excellent school may continue. The need is indicated when we say that the schoolroom is pitifully small and several applications have had to be turned down on this account.' (*Sheffield Times*)

MAY 6TH

1862: On this day, one of the most violent storms in living memory occurred. Before 5 p.m., the sky began to darken and, by 6 p.m., it was as black as night. The rain mingled with hailstones, descended in torrents and the wind rose, blowing a violent gale from the south. One witness at Attercliffe claims he picked up a hailstone which was an inch and a half in circumference and three quarters of an inch thick. The railway trains were considerably delayed during the evening by the storm. The large sash windows of a public house belonging to John Backhouse of the High Street in Attercliffe, were blown in. Lightning struck the house of Mr Willington, surgeon, who lived in a house at the corner of Eyre Street and Charles Street. It would appear that the lightning seems to have entered the servant's bedroom via the chimney, sending a great quantity of soot and dirt into the room. An outside wall was also damaged; a young woman was letting down her umbrella to enter her house and was struck on the cheek by a piece of stone which shattered from the wall. Gradually the storm died down, and, by 9 p.m., peace was returned. (*Sheffield Times*)

MAY 7TH

1899: The famous circus act of Barnum and Bailey came to Sheffield. It was their second visit to the town and on previous visits it was all the people of the town could talk about. The circus company bedded down on the old Queens Hotel grounds on Langsett Road. The show had been based at Nottingham and the previous night they packed up a total of 103 wagons, 840 people, 430 horses and ponies, and twenty-five cages of wild animals, including twenty elephants, eighteen camels and four zebras. Despite the early hour of the morning, the roads were lined with people to watch the event and the circus reached the Queens Hotel grounds at 4.30 a.m. By 10 a.m., the circus big top and most of the other tents had been erected. The *Sheffield Independent* reporter was told that familiar freaks would re-appear under the name of 'prodigies', including Hassan Ali, the Egyptian giant who stood at an impressive 7ft 11in in height. The show would also include Miss Oguri Kiba, an armless Japanese lady, whose act involved doing things with her feet that people normally do with their hands. (*Sheffield Independent*)

MAY 8TH

1858: A lecture was delivered by the Revd Brewin Grant BA in Ranmoor School room on the subject of India. The lecturer, who had visited the country on many occasions, discussed the history of India, its environment and culture. He also pointed out some of the prominent features proceeding and attending the present mutiny. He explored what benefits England might reap from India if it were properly governed and if the opium trade was abolished and cotton cultivated in its place. He then proceeded to show what effects this would have on the American slave trade. The lecture, which lasted for an hour and a half, was of the most interesting description, and although the room was uncomfortably crowded, it was listened to with great attention. At the conclusion, some pleasant remarks were made by the chairman (Mr Bingham) to thank Revd Grant for his most entertaining lecture. Mr Rhodes spoke about the desirability of having other similar lectures during the summer months. Revd Grant promised his support to such efforts and a committee was formed for the purpose of carrying out these arrangements. The whole evening ended with a prayer followed by refreshments. (*Sheffield Times*)

MAY 9TH

1849: Today's newspaper contained a report on a 'witch doctor' in Sheffield and an alleged case of maltreatment. An inquest had been held on the death of Richard Lindley, a mattress maker (48), who, having suffered from disease of the lungs and chest for some years, died rather suddenly on the previous Thursday. He had been treated by John Brierley, who was known as the 'Halifax Witch'. Described as a man 'whose ignorance is only to be equalled by the gullibility of the almost incredible numbers who have flocked to his rooms at a Tavern in Townhead Street', Brierley told the inquest that he had never been trained and had started 'doctoring' at twelve years of age and had continued to do so for twenty-eight years. Brierley's diagnosis was that Lindley's heart was three inches out of place. Lindley's own doctor, Mr Henry Payne, appeared at the inquest and told the coroner that he had treated him for various chest complaints over the last five years. When he completed the post-mortem, he found that the lungs and liver were diseased, but that the heart was in its proper place. The jury recorded a verdict of death from pulmonary apoplexy. (*Sheffield Independent*)

MAY 10TH

1847: The Sheffield Workhouse drew up a list of regulations which was published today:

> That for the future, all applications for an apprentice will be made to the master.
>
> If a selection be made, the name and address of the party applying shall be taken down and forwarded to the district relieving officer, who shall be required to visit the house of the person requiring an apprentice, and be prepared to report, on the following board day, the information he had obtained, in the presence of the boy and his proposed master.
>
> Should the board determine the offer of apprenticeship to be satisfactory, then the relieving officer shall enter in his application book the boys name for a change of linen and the boy shall go on trial for one month. At the end of which, the boy shall either be delivered up by his master to the relieving officer, or give notice to the clerk of the union of his desire to have the boy bound as an apprentice.
>
> In the latter case, the clerk shall prepare the indentures for presentation to the board in the presence of all parties concerned.

(Bunker, B., *Portrait of Sheffield* (London, Hale Publishing, 1972)

MAY 11TH

1820: It was reported at the previous town meeting, that, as Mr John Waterfall had been appointed one of the acting constables, as a consequence Mr Jeremiah Sayno was elected town beadle in his place. Sayno was told that he had to wear the town livery on all public occasions, and when in attendance on business for the town trustees. The trust had agreed that the beadle's wife and two children were allowed to reside with him in his own apartments within the Town Hall. Sayno was ordered to behave properly and respectfully at all times, whether on town business or in his own time. He was also instructed that if he did not comply with these requisitions, he would be subject to immediate dismissal. In such circumstances, he shall be required to give up his office and quit the Town Hall premises within one calendar month's notice from the Trustees, or from their collectors. For the time being, Sayno was instructed that he had to deliver notices for public meetings in and around the town centre and also attend them. (Leader, J.D., *The Records of the Burgery of Sheffield*, Sheffield Independent Press, 1897)

MAY 12TH

1860: The trade report printed on this day stated that there was an 'almost universal flatness' which seemed to pervade all manufacturing houses. There was a marked decrease in the weight of goods dispatched from the railway stations and the table knife trade was reported as 'very slack'. The reporter stated that: 'the steel manufacturers have no reason at present to complain about the state of their orders, but we have heard that there is still not quite so much doing even in this branch, owing principally to a falling off of orders from America. The arrival of a few East India orders has created a little more activity in the saw trade, however, and the orders for crinoline steel are coming in satisfactorily. All the machine and engineer tool makers appear to be very busy indeed, which is a sure sign that the superior quality of the goods made here is more and more appreciated. The dispute with the grinder in the stove trade remains, we regret to say, in an unsatisfactory state. Such is the state at the moment in Sheffield we can only pray that soon an upturn in orders are being received, will ensure our manufacturers are working full steam once more'. (*Daily Telegraph*)

MAY 13TH

1870: An inspection of the Borough Police Force was held today at the Bramall Lane grounds by Captain Elgee, the government inspector. The men were ordered to parade at 10 a.m. and appeared on the ground punctually. The force comprised of one chief constable, two superintendents, eight inspectors, seven sub inspectors, ten detectives, eighteen sergeants and 180 constables – making a total of 226 on parade. There were also present, in addition to the Inspector and Mr Jackson the chief constable, members of the Watch Committee. After Captain Elgee inspected the men, their clothing and their appointments, he inspected their drill, which was carried out under the command of the chief constable. The men marched past in slow and quick time and went through a variety of other movements, the police band playing lively music. At the conclusion of the manoeuvres, Captain Elgee expressed great satisfaction at the appearance and deportment of the force, of which he intended to report very favourably. The men were then dismissed from the ground and Captain Elgee, accompanied by the chief constable, extended his tour of inspection to the central police office and the station at Highfields. In both cases he congratulated the chief constable on the arrangements. (*Sheffield Post*)

MAY 14TH

1850: On this day, the death of a horse from hydrophobia occurred at Royds Hall farm. It seems that about a month previously, a carter employed by the company had been given a dog from the gamekeeper of Kirklees Hall. The carter tied the dog to the rear of his cart, and, on reaching Royds Hall, he let the dog loose; almost immediately, it ran away and bit a child. After being deflected by the child's father, the dog then bit the horse that was pulling the cart on the nose, later escaping. About ten or twelve days prior to the horse's death, it began to suffer from distressing symptoms and when the vet, Mr Byron, called to see the horse, he declared it was hydrophobia. The poor creature was a sorry sight to behold, running open-mouthed at every object in its reach and being evidently in great distress and agony. A messenger had been dispatched to the home of Mr Waterton, who had a celebrated prescription to cure the disease, but the messenger found that he was not at home and was in fact in Belgium. The horse, which had been valued at between £20 and £25, soon after died. (*Sheffield Independent*)

MAY 15TH

1874: A meeting of the disgruntled agricultural labourers was held at the bottom of Pinfold Lane, Attercliffe. Councillor Skelton took the chair and, addressing the huge crowd, told them that he had some experience amongst the agricultural labourers. He thought they were the worst paid, worst fed, worst clad and worst educated class of people in existence. In many cases, the only hope in old age was death in a workhouse and a pauper funeral. On the other hand, they could scarcely find a better fed and clothed class of men than the local farmers. They had everything they desired to make them happy and comfortable. They rode to market in carriages, which were good enough for Fitzwilliam (the local Earl), and they died rich men. He thought the time was not far distant when the agricultural labourers must advance their position in society. He thought that the tyrannical farmers of Sheffield and the neighbourhood ought not to be allowed to drive labourers out of their tied cottages. Other addresses were delivered by delegates from the Labourers union, and a unanimous vote of sympathy to the striking agricultural labourers was eventually passed. (*Daily Telegraph*)

MAY 16TH

1845: The annual Whitsuntide visit to Rotherham was marred by the lack of trains back to Sheffield. It seems that on Sunday night, between two and three hundred 'pleasure passengers' had been unable to return back to Sheffield following a visit to the Rotherham Fair after the last train had left the station. A message was sent for another train, but, when it reached 10.30 p.m., people were forced to make their own travel arrangements. Some lucky people obtained lodgings in Rotherham, others found shelter for their children and were then forced to walk the six miles home. With this in mind, it would have been thought that arrangements for Monday night would have improved, but it was equally disastrous. Instead of one train every half hour, it seems to have been running every hour and a half. A reporter arrived at 7 p.m. to find a large crowd of people outside the station at Rotherham. At 8 p.m., there was a crush of people on the platforms, but no engine. As each carriage was turned and pushed on to join the train, there was a scramble to get into it, until the finally engine arrived at 9 p.m. to return to Sheffield. (*Sheffield Mercury*)

MAY 17TH

1867: On this day, an assault was made on Alderman Saunders, the chair of the board of Sheffield Workhouse guardians, by William Sixton and Thomas Langstaff. Sixton had been a former inmate of the workhouse, who had been taken before the guardians on the previous Monday and told to leave as he was single, able-bodied and had work offered to him. He refused to leave and it was only the day before that he was finally turned out of the workhouse. That same morning, at about 8.40 a.m., the two men had gone to the house belonging to Alderman Saunders and demanded re-admittance to the workhouse, claiming that they had been unable to get any work. Alderman Saunders told Sixton that he was unable to allow him to re-enter, and Sixton swung a punch at him. Fortunately, Saunders put up his arm to block the blow, and then managed to step back into his house and closed the door. Sixton and Langstaff hung around the garden, obviously waiting for Saunders to reappear. However, Saunders managed to escape and bring a police constable back to his house. Both Sixton and Langstaff were then taken into custody but Saunders asked that Langstaff be released as he had not shown any violence towards him. (*Sheffield Independent*)

MAY 18TH

1891: A newspaper on this day contained an account of a German 'Baron' who was charged with travelling on the Midland Railway without having paid his fare, and with intent to avoid payment. Paul von Knobloch, who described himself as a German 'Baron', was stopped by a ticket collector at Heeley Station in a carriage on the train from Chesterfield to Sheffield. He presented a ticket which was from Chesterfield to Sheepbridge, and, when asked to pay the difference, he claimed that he had no money. He had paid for as far as he could go and intended to travel on until he was stopped. He told the ticket collector that he wanted to get to Sheffield. Another person in the carriage told him that if he offered the ticket collector the parcel he was carrying, as a guarantee that he would pay, he could go on his way. However, Knobloch refused to give up the parcel. The prisoner, who was described as being in a poor and shabby condition, declared himself to be guilty and 'asked for punishment'. The Bench fined him 40s, including costs, the alternative being one months' imprisonment. The prisoner was unable to pay and so was escortedto the cells. (*Sheffield Independent*)

MAY 19TH

1839: Sheffield was today described as being 'in a bit of a bustle' as Chartists from Rotherham were joined by Chartists from Sheffield in an open-air meeting at Paradise Square. The *Sheffield Iris* reported that the meeting was of the 'greatest order, harmony and peace', rendering useless the special constables appointed to be in readiness in case of a riot. Speakers were generally dismissive of the workhouse system, as they deprecated the Poor Law centralized system. One of the speakers had spent eleven weeks and three days in a workhouse, which he referred to as a 'bastille', and he went into lengthy detail of the diet and the treatment whilst inside. The inmates had worked at grinding meal from 7 a.m. to 6 p.m. and were fed chiefly on gruel. The family, consisting of himself, his wife, his son and daughter, were all put into separate wards. He spoke about an elderly woman, who had been persecuted by the master of the workhouse and put into a 'black hole' for 24 hours, without anything to eat and no shoes on. His complaints about the workhouse system were met with cheers and applause from an audience of around two thousand people. (*Sheffield Iris*)

MAY 20TH

1919: King George V and Queen Mary visited Sheffield on this day, and were cheered by tens of thousands of revellers who had all been set free for a day from work. The last time the Royal couple visited Sheffield was during the war, when they found the city straining to provide sorely needed munitions. On that occasion, busy men and women could do no more than run into the streets for a few minutes, to offer a loyal greeting before returning to the benches and the lathes. His Majesty told the assembled crowds: 'It is with the greatest possible pleasure that the Queen and I renew our acquaintance with the City of Sheffield, and we thank you for the loyal and dutiful address with which you have welcomed us. We come to you at the joyful and auspicious moment when the country is emerging from the long night of war, and is looking forward to the dawn of the day of peace.' Two hundred former soldiers were inspected by the King and although they wore civilian clothing, they had all, without exception, served abroad during the Great War. The King then stood on the steps of the Town Hall to take the salute of thousands of soldiers and demobilized men as they marched eight abreast. (*The Times*)

May 21st

1873: It was reported in today's *Evening Star* that a man who had burgled several houses in and around Yorkshire had been captured in Sheffield on the previous Saturday afternoon. He was described as an inoffensive man who had latterly gone by the name of William Pitt. A reward of £100 had been given for the arrest of Pitt, who was thought to have committed several burglaries in Sheffield which had remained unsolved. At 2.30 p.m., PC W. Stone saw him enter a pawnbrokers' shop on West Bar, and, when he exited, Stone asked him to accompany him to the police station. He was interviewed by Inspector Mackley and finally told the officers where he had been staying. The police and prisoner went to the lodgings in Solly Street and, in the attic, they found over 100 articles of considerable value, including watches, brooches, lockets, cigar cases, scent bottles and other trinkets. The reporter states that: 'It is thought that the man who had been entering numerous mansions and halls by the score, and almost every detective's pocket book has contained his portrait, he succeeded in escaping the vigilance until apprehended by an ordinary Sheffield policeman.' (*Evening Star*)

MAY 22ND

1850: It was reported that a nightingale was heard on the outskirts of Sheffield. The reporter stated that: 'We were stopped in our lonely path, and riveted to the spot for upwards of half an hour by that wonderful songster, the nightingale. To mention the precise locality would be to advertise for its capture, which no real lover of nature would think of doing. It is well known to those who are observant of the songs of our native warblers that either from age or other circumstances, different individuals have different powers of execution. The bird alluded to, executed in perfection all the wondrous staves which have won for it the admiration and surprise of every British naturalist. The loudness, fullness and richness of the tone we have never known to be exceeded. In short it was one of the richest treats that can be conceived. But as the season is far advanced, we fear it is almost too late to go again with anything like certainty of hearing it in full song; for the wants of his family will be, in future, too pressing to give him much time for filling the woodlands with his rich melody.' (*Sheffield Independent*)

MAY 23RD

1842: Details of an inquest were printed in the newspapers today. The inquest had been held on the death of William Hague, an illegitimate child who lived in Ecclesfield Workhouse. The ten-week-old child had been found dead in bed with his mother on the morning of May 22nd. It appeared from the evidence that another woman, Martha Beardshaw, and two other children were all sleeping in the same bed. The workhouse master informed the coroner that at the time there were twenty-four males, twenty-seven females and forty-one children in the house, besides the master and matron; making ninety-four persons. The sleeping accommodation consisted of twenty-nine beds, and many of the rooms were small and poorly ventilated. Nine children had been suffering from whooping cough and two had died of that disease. There were seven males, eight females and eleven children sick in the workhouse at this moment. The coroner stated that under such circumstances, he was not surprised that a child should be found dead in bed and the jury returned a verdict 'that the deceased was found dead in bed without marks of violence, having been accidentally overlaid or suffocated.' (*Sheffield Iris*)

MAY 24TH

1831: An inquest was held on the death of a young man, who married and died on the same day. The coroner, Mr Thomas Badger, held an inquest at the Punch Bowl Inn, South Street, Sheffield Moor on John Vardy (whose 19th birthday had been held on March 5th). On the previous day he had married his sweetheart, Mary Richards (also 19), at Rotherham. Several witnesses at the wedding gave evidence to the coroner and the jury of the events leading up to the death. It seems that the wedding party had returned back to Sheffield, and had spent the day happily at the house of the bride's father, Mr Richards. The new bride retired to bed about 11 p.m. and, shortly afterwards, was joined by her new husband. The couple had both been reported as merry and cheerful throughout the day. The bridegroom was sober when he retired to bed with his wife. Within a short period of only five or ten minutes, however, he had a fit of apoplexy and expired in his new wife's arms. A surgeon was called, but the man was dead before he arrived. (*The Standard*)

MAY 25TH

1830: The authorities were informed on this day that a man lay dead in a house near the Haymarket; his friends were preparing to bury him, although the circumstances attending his death demanded investigation. PCs Wild and Waterfall immediately proceeded to a small tenement at the back of Mr Tasker's public house and, in a low apartment, placed on a sort of settee, they found the body of Richard Gibbons, a working saddler. The fifty-year-old appeared to have passed but a short time before, yet his body had swelled to an enormous size; this could only mean that death occurred through unnatural causes. A jury was summoned later on that day, and it was evident that the deceased had met his death in consequence of drinking an excessive quantity of rum. The coroner remarked with much severity on the conduct of a companion of the deceased, who had been heard to say whilst drinking with Gibbons that he would kill him; his expression at this point suggested that he would force or tempt him to consume liquor sufficient to cause death. The jury returned a verdict 'that the deceased Richard Gibbons met his death in consequence of excessive drinking'. (*Sheffield Iris*)

MAY 26TH

1863: A public meeting was held in Paradise Square by Mr Roebuck Esq. The meeting concerned Britain's recognition of the Confederate States of America, and was printed in the local newspaper today. He asked the crowd of between 6,000 and 8,000 people to sign a memorial to 'request Her Majesty's government to use its good offices to procure a suspension of hostilities in the state of North America, for a settlement of the question of the issues betwixt them'. So many people attended the meeting that many were forced to sit on the steps reserved for the speakers. The Mayor, John Bramley Esq., had difficulty in climbing the steps to open the meeting! Despite the crowds, it was reported that the people were very orderly and supported the resolution. Many queued up to sign the memorial and Mr Roebuck made arrangements for it to be sent to London that very day. The memorial also requested that the government immediately enter into negotiations with the great powers of Europe to acknowledge the independence of the Confederate state of North America. The meeting, which continued for over three hours, held a large proportion of middle-class men than was considered usual in such gatherings. (*Sheffield Independent*)

MAY 27TH

1862: Today the *Sheffield Times* published the names and details of some of the tradesmen of Sheffield who were exhibiting their goods at the International Exhibition in London. It was, after the Crystal Palace exhibition, one of the best showcases for industry technology and arts, and was held in South Kensington on the site of the present Natural History Museum. The reporter claimed that:

> I now proceed to give you readers some account of the lighter class of cutlery in the Exhibition…which are goods of all orders of society. Scissors, pens and pocket knives are everybody companions and table cutlery of daily use.
>
> H.C. Booth and Co., Norfolk Works, Sheffield show an assortment of goods varying in style and quality.
>
> J. Drabble and Co., Orchard Works, Sheffield: There is nothing particularly noticeable about their goods, unless it is the machine which facilitate the production.
>
> J. Gibbings and Sons, Sheffield exhibit a case of fine scissors and penknives. For a small display there is nothing in the whole court to surpass the articles shown by this fine house.

Featuring over 28,000 exhibitors from thirty-six countries, which attracted over six million visitors, the city of Sheffield was proud to be included in this magnificent exhibition. (*Sheffield Times*)

MAY 28TH

1862: The celebrated M. Blondin (the hero of Niagara) gave a stunning tightrope-walking performance at the Newhall Gardens today, on his second visit to Sheffield. Using a rope 100 yards long and 60ft high, which was anchored to the ground by sandbags, he commenced his performance by walking backwards and forwards across the rope, carrying a pole. Having succeeded, he received a rapturous applause from the audience. His next trick was to walk the rope again – on this occasion, however, he was blindfolded. During one part of the act, he stood on his head on the rope and he also lay flat across it; he performed with great confidence, making it look as easy as if he was doing it on the ground. Blondin then crossed the rope with a sack over his head, which extended down to his knees. His confident nature throughout the performance drew many cheers and exclamations from the crowd. Blondin completed his performance by carrying a man weighing 12 stone in piggyback fashion across the rope, once again to magnificent applause. The management claimed that there were over 10,000 spectators, many of which came on special trains from Birmingham and other places. (*The Telegraph*)

MAY 29TH

1857: An action to recover money totalling £250 was heard in the Court of the Queens Bench before of Mr Justice Wightman at York. In March 1856, Mr Cavill purchased the plant of the *Sheffield Free Press*. He was to have deposited £250 as a surety that the rest of the money would be paid. The seller, Mr Ironside, was willing to dispense with the actual cash and agreed to an IOU to be paid the following week. Instead, Cavill repudiated the bargain and in order to forfeit having to pay the surety, sold up and absconded from Sheffield. It seems that he had arranged for a passage on a vessel about to sail for Australia when he was captured. The judge called on his solicitor to ask what possible defence he was going to give. His defence, Mr Deighton, told him that the IOU had been demanded on March 7th, whereas in actual fact it was not due until March 14th. His Lordship asked Deighton 'if his client had re-paid the money', and was told that he hadn't. The judge said, 'My judgement is decidedly against you.' He then ordered Mr Cavill to pay the court costs in addition to the money he owed. (*Sheffield Free Press*)

MAY 30TH

1839: On this day, the Botanical Gardens received a very prestigious visitor. It was announced that Mr J.C. London, the able contributor to such eminent editions as the *Gardeners Magazine* and the *Agricultural Magazine*, visited the Botanical Gardens. The reporter stated that: 'We understand that he has expressed great approbation of the formation of the Gardens and he said that he considered for the beauty of its situation, and for the elegance and extent of the conservatories, they were unequalled in his experience'. Offering his thanks to the Mayor for the enthusiastic welcome he had received, Mr London justly remarked that the whole kingdom would cry 'shame' upon the people of Sheffield, if, having provided such Gardens, they failed to support them. Only a few years earlier, there had been a movement to get rid of the Botanical Gardens, but thankfully a subscription list was started and the Gardens saved. Also anticipated was that the list would be considerably augmented by the tradesmen and manufacturers of Sheffield, and that the prominent men of the town would offer their themselves to subscribe to the Gardens in a manner creditable to the town. (*Sheffield Independent*)

MAY 31ST

1886: A report of a domestic servant who had been brought to the police court, charged with stealing a calico bag and some Christmas cards, featured heavily in the newspapers on this day. Sarah Ann Lloyd (18) had been brought to court by her mistress Mrs Murphy, who employed her at her home on Durham Road. She told the court that the prisoner had been in her service for just eighteen days prior to her being sacked. Suspecting Lloyd of the theft of some of her belongings, the girl's box was searched and the stolen items found. The Mayor asked Mrs Murphy why she pressed for punishment in the case, and she told him it was because of the 'vile abuse' that she had been subjected to by Lloyd. The stepmother of the girl came forward and stated that she could not defend the girl, and that 'her father did not care what became of her, as she was such a bad girl'. The Mayor stated it would be better to take her home and show her some kindness. The girl was fined 5s and dismissed. (*Sheffield Post*)

JUNE 1ST

1869: A meeting was held today on the subject of the rebuilding of the Sheffield Ragged School, which had been destroyed in a fire. The Mayor presided over the meeting and he started by giving such statistics in order to prove what the school had achieved in the past. He felt that the school should be rebuilt, saying: 'In many large towns, half the children were running about the streets and not learning anything. That is certainly the case in Sheffield and by attending the school the object is to rescue these children and train them in paths of usefulness and diligence. I am of the opinion that the working classes might spare a few pence for several consecutive weeks, against the rebuilding of the school'. Revd Stainton said that many of the children who had attended the Ragged School in the past were orphans, and others were members of large families whose parents were poor and unable to properly care for them. A resolution was then made that a subscription be started towards the building of a new Ragged School. (*Sheffield Times*)

JUNE 2ND

1831: Three people – Susan Day, Edward Rowbotham and John Oates were arrested for stealing today. Inspector Bland told the magistrate that he had acquired some information that the female prisoner kept a house in West Bar for the reception of thieves and stolen goods, and that he went there between 1 a.m. and 2 a.m. for the purpose of examining the property. He proceeded into the bed chamber, where there was not the least bit of furniture, and on three heaps of straw he found no fewer than thirteen young lads. He knew that at least five or six of them had been at Wakefield Gaol. During the search, he had found a quantity of stolen pots. A respectable-looking female at the house had said she was the mother of one of the boys. The female prisoner had harboured him for more than a fortnight past, and when she went to fetch him away, there were nearly a dozen girls in the house who threatened her if she did not go about her business. Inspector Bland exclaimed, 'I have had nearly twenty years' experience, and this is the worst hole I ever saw in my life'. Each of the prisoners was sentenced to three months' imprisonment. (*Sheffield Iris*)

JUNE 3RD

1882: A meeting of Sheffield Music Hall proprietors and professional artists was held today at the Gaiety Hall, on West Bar. The purpose of the meeting was to raise a subscription for the assistance of the company, who had been engaged at the Alhambra Music Hall when a fire had occurred. Mr Dale, a member of the company, stated that the cast had lost all they had, but the most serious loss was that of the sheet music, which would be difficult to replace. Some of the professionals were now penniless, having lost all their property. Several of the music halls in the town, including the Theatre of Varieties, the Gaiety, the Fleur de Lis and the Star Music Hall, had all agreed to give free benefits for the sufferers. It was expected that the lessees of the Theatre Royal and the Alexandra would do the same. It was decided to forward the subscription lists to all the leading provincial halls, where it was anticipated that these would be met with a liberal response. The origins of the fire still remained a mystery. *(Evening Star)*

JUNE 4TH

1874: A letter was sent to the editor of the *Sheffield Independent* today which condemned the state of the streets of Sheffield:

June 4th 1874

Sir,

Can you inform me how it is that our main thoroughfares and wholesale markets are always in such a dirty state? The amount of horse manure and other refuse that is allowed to accumulate is a disgrace to our town, and would not, I am convinced, be allowed in many places of less importance. Anyone who is in the habit of visiting London occasionally, as I am, cannot fail to notice how clean the streets and causeways are kept. I am aware that the atmosphere of our town must necessarily be black and sooty, by reason of the various trades carried out requiring fire; but surely, Mr Editor, there is no reason why our streets should be left in such a filthy condition. Perhaps the gentlemen representing the Highway Committee agree with that townsman of ours who is said to prefer the air of Sheffield to that of the seaside, as there is more 'body' in it. I remain dear Sir, yours respectfully, signed SCAVENGER.

(*Sheffield Independent*)

JUNE 5TH

1840: An adjourned inquest featured in the newspapers today. Held on the evening of June 4th, the death of Ellen Wright (43) was subject to examination – she died during the previous week in childbirth. The first inquest had been heard at the Warm Hearthstone Inn on Townhead Street before the coroner, Mr T. Badger. It appears that the deceased had gone into labour and was attended by a midwife named Mary Richardson, who had practiced for over fourteen years. The case became complicated and medical aid was sought at about midnight, but, before any assistance could arrive, the woman died before she could deliver the baby. The case was adjourned last evening at Mr Badger's office, when the midwife was examined in close detail regarding her experience. Medical men were examined as to her practice and behaviour, which was deemed to be suitable. Other mothers gave evidence of the care that they had received at the hands of Mrs Richardson. The jury was sent into another room in order to consider their verdict. After an absence of one hour, they finally stated that in their opinion Ellen Wright had died from a hard labour. The coroner agreed but he criticised Mary Richardson for not calling in medical assistance sooner. (*Sheffield Iris*)

JUNE 6TH

1871: A case of bigamy committed by a former resident of Sheffield was heard today. The case, which was held at Cambridge, concerned a man named John Bewley who had worked as an assistant for Mr Proctor – draper of Fargate, Sheffield. Next door to the shop lived Mr Proctor's niece, Margaret Stothart, the eldest daughter of Mr M. Stothart, iron founder at Cambridge. Bewley represented himself as a single man and, forgetting about his wife and five children in Scotland, started a courtship with Miss Stothart. Her father, on his deathbed, gave his permission for the two of them to marry and the ceremony was performed at the registry office at Cambridge by special license on April 2nd 1870. Shortly after the marriage, Bewley visited his wife and children in Penrith and continued a warm correspondence with her. Upon Miss Stothart's father's death, Bewley took over the business and things went well until rumours of his bigamy began to circulate in the town. He confessed all to his new 'wife' and then absconded to London. He contacted his first wife and she wrote to him care of a box number, and he agreed to meet her on Stirbitch Common; however, it was here that he was swiftly arrested and sent to the assizes. (*Sheffield Daily Telegraph*)

JUNE 7TH

1876: Today was the first day of a sale, which would last for four days, of a collection of illuminated manuscripts of great value and importance to the people of Sheffield. The manuscripts had been exhibited to the public on a number of occasions. The collection belonged to Mr Bragge of Sheffield, who managed the Atlas Steelworks, which began twenty-five years ago in order to obtain specimens of calligraphy. After travelling all over the world in search of his favourite objects, he was in the possession of a collection of over 500 books and manuscripts, which were described as being 'of first rate excellence'. Much of the collection was in a state of fine preservation, and some were still wrapped in their splendid old bindings. The manuscripts and books, which amounted to over 491 'lots', were sold at the rooms of Messrs Sotheby, Wilkinson and Hodge in London. The interest in the sale could clearly be seen from the large number of people who were bidding, and *The Times* remarked that that such a curious and extensive a private collection had rarely been seen in the salerooms of London. The sale realised a total of £12,272 at the end of four days. (*The Times*)

JUNE 8TH

1871: A robbery was committed and the two villains were caught on this day. About noon, the shop of Mr George Lief, a pawnbroker of Church Street, was quite busy. Some children near the door, waiting for their parents inside the shop, observed two men looking in the window. Presently and without warning, one of the men smashed the window and breaking a pane of glass – whilst the other made a grab for some watches that were hanging up inside. Mr Lief's attention was attracted by the noise and on going to the door, the children informed him of what they had seen. On examining the window, it was found that only one gold watch had been taken. Information was at once given to the police. About three quarters of an hour after the robbery had been committed, PC Gregory saw two men in Gibraltar Street whose appearance corresponded so exactly to the description given of the robbers, that he took them into custody and the gold watch was found on one of them. The men gave the names of George Thompson of Warrington and William Cowan of Manchester. They appeared before the magistrate the following day. (*Sheffield Times*)

JUNE 9TH

1829: This morning some members of the Anti-Slavery Society gathered at the Manor Court room on Brown Street to meet the Revd Dr Phillips, an independent missionary to the south of Africa. The Revd Gentleman discussed in great detail the demoralising effects of slavery which greatly hindered the spread of the Gospel, in particular areas of Africa. He told the audience that there were at least 100,000 souls taken annually from the coast of Africa for the purpose of slavery, of whom around 5,000 were murdered. This system was likely to continue whilst £20,000 to £40,000 profit was realised by a cargo of slaves. There were in the House of Commons in 1829, sixty-seven proprietors of slaves, twenty holders of West Indian bonds, and 200 individuals who were connected to slave proprietors by marriage or otherwise. Dr Phillips recommended the disuse of West Indian sugar in Sheffield until they had accomplished not only amelioration, but a total abolition of slavery. Revd William Watson asked Dr Phillips what the Sheffield Society could do to aid the London Slavery Society. Dr Phillips recommended petitioning to the House of Commons from all parts of the kingdom. The resolution to do so was carried unanimously. (*Sheffield Independent*)

JUNE 10TH

1876: Today, an illuminated address was presented to Alderman Mark Firth as gratitude for his presentation of Firth Park to the people of Sheffield. He had made this generous present of the deeds on September 8th 1875 to the Corporation and their successors. It was recorded that the park was to be used by the public for the recreation of the inhabitants of Sheffield. It had also been arranged that their Royal Highnesses, the Prince and Princess of Wales, would opened the park on August 10th 1875. At that time Mr Firth was Mayor of Sheffield, and during the ceremony, the Mayor handed the Prince of Wales the deeds, which were then placed in the hands of the Town Clerk. The illuminated address was handsomely bound in a volume, on which was engraved the town arms. The address presented to Alderman Firth read, 'this noble gift and his other munificent acts have caused his name to be regarded with honour and love by the people of Sheffield.' The address was signed by John Yeomans, the Town Clerk, and it was announced that the illuminated address would be exhibited the following week in Weston Park Museum. (*Sheffield Post*)

JUNE 11TH

1832: The corner stone of the new Cutler's Hall was laid today by the Master Cutler, James Blake Esq. The ceremony was attended by the Cutler's Company and Mr J. Wilson, the clerk, Revd J. Blackburn, the Sheffield chaplain, Mr Samuel Worth and Mr Benjamin Broomhead Taylor, both architects, as well as a number of principle gentlemen of the town. Beneath the stone were placed a number of coins, specimens of the existing state of the town's manufacture (cutlery only), and newspapers and records of the existing year. After the business of the morning, the Cutler's Company and others dined at the Tontine Inn. The estimated cost of the new building was said to be £6,500 and was to be the third Cutler's Hall to be erected on the site of the previous buildings, which had been erected in 1638 and 1725. The plans showed a Corinthian frontage, behind which was a series of different rooms, one of which displayed knives made in Sheffield during the Elizabethan period. Many of these were found by mud larks (Victorian children who scavenged the mud) working in the tidal mud of the River Thames in London. (Leader, R., *Sheffield Local Directory*, Sheffield Independent Press, 1897)

JUNE 12TH

1831: The *Sheffield Independent* gave an account of an order for cutlery that had been completed for their Majesty's King William IV and Queen Adelaide, by Sheffield cutlers Messrs Sanson & Sons. The order consisted of a complete set of table and desert knives and forks in two handsome mahogany cases, inlaid with silver. The blades of the knives were of the finest cast steel and the handles were of ivory, ornamented with an engraved crown. The ferules were of silver, chased with the rose, thistle and shamrock. The forks were made in the English fashion of silver and had four prongs. The reporter stated: 'It must be gratifying to our Sheffield readers to learn that the King has directed that they should be made with handles that correspond with the knives. The desert knives and forks are made in the same manner. This elegant service has been made by the express order of his Majesty and according to the pattern selected by himself. This, it may be presumed, will set at rest the question which has been raised of "who are the King's cutler?" If any persons can claim that honour it must be those who can produce the warrant of their appointment and who receive and execute orders for their Majesty's and their household.' (*Sheffield Independent*)

JUNE 13TH

1851: A report on how the people of Sheffield spent the Whitsuntide holiday, which was looked forward to 'by all the classes of society', was published today. The reporter stated that: 'On every side of Sheffield are places to visit such as Wharncliffe with its magnificent woods, shady walks and precipitous rocks, Wentworth with its noble mansion and extensive park and Worksop with its manorial ruins, its ducal residence and it beautiful scenery. These places have been brought to our doors by the railways and there are always holiday excursions at fares too temptingly low to be resisted. In this fashion, on Monday 800 people visited Wharncliffe and a special train on the Manchester, Sheffield and Lincolnshire Railway carried 1,400 people to Manchester, Liverpool and the Isle of Man. Crowds of these visitors flocked to the station to begin the day's excursions. Other destinations were Haddon Hall, with its picturesque and antiquated buildings; Chatsworth, the famed palace of the Peak; Roche Abbey with its ruins.' It was reported that the trains were so crowded that many travellers didn't get back to Sheffield until late at night, but they were no doubt refreshed with their day away. (*Sheffield Free Press*)

JUNE 14TH

1828: On this day was published an account of several evenings of recitation, which had been given by Mr Clarke at the Town Hall illustrating the principles of elocution, particularly involving the cure of impediments of speech. The *Sheffield Iris* states that on Wednesday evening, to demonstrate these principles, a young gentleman about twenty years of age, a pupil of Mr Clarke, attempted before the audience to read a sentence from a random volume offered to him by a bystander. The young man could barely utter three words without stammering to such a degree that was painful to watch. However, Mr Clarke stated that in just two days he could have this young man reading fluently. The crowd was amazed on Thursday to see the same gentleman read for a considerable time without hesitation. Such was the improvement in his confidence that he was able to answer any questions asked him with fluency and ease. The *Iris* stated: 'Having witnessed the extraordinary progress of this individual, we think that all parents and guardians who have young persons under their control afflicted with impediments of speech, would not do them justice if they let such an opportunity slip of having them so readily cured.' (*Sheffield Iris*)

JUNE 15TH

1839: This morning, a prize fighter named Benjamin Bennison was brought before the magistrates. The previous evening evidence was placed before the police that a prize fight for £10 was to be fought the next day. The chief constable urged PCs Wild and Bland to stop this fight by any means and to find the two men involved. The constables received this information about 11 p.m. and immediately went in search of the named parties. At an early hour of the morning of June 15th, they brought Bennison into custody after he was arrested at a house in Snow Hill, Park. They had, as yet, not found the other combatant, named as John Morton, and, as a result of this, the case had to be adjourned. The reporter for the *Sheffield Independent* stated, 'We are thus indebted to the prompt attention of the worthy magistrate, and the exertions of the police officers for the prevention of a scene disgraceful to the neighbourhood'. However, he later stated that, 'We have lately been told that at the time of going to print Morton has since been arrested'. (*Sheffield Independent*)

JUNE 16TH

1857: A visit from the Cooke's Equestrian Company was reported today, who gave a performance in the cattle market. Audiences watched in fascination as the feats the Equestrian Company achieved elicited frequent manifestations of approbation. During their stay in Sheffield, it was reported that the company had been so unfortunate as to lose one of their most valuable horses. Immediately the animal showed symptoms of suffering it was placed under the care of Mr Cartledge, the veterinary surgeon. It seems that the suffering arose from a rupture of the stomach and it was clear that the horse was dying. The reason for the death was that the animal had been trained to sit upon its haunches during the performance of some of its tricks, and so strong is the force of habit, it had come to prefer that mode of taking rest to the customary equine mode of lying down. It was also reported to have sat on its haunches when eating its corn. When Mr Cartledge went to examine the horse, he found it in that posture, in which it remained to the last. The animal was blind but nonetheless valuable to the company. (*Sheffield Free Press*)

JUNE 17TH

1895: The Sheffield Journal today printed a report on a suicide. A girl named Emily Smith (16), whose parents lived in Amy Street, Sheffield, committed suicide yesterday morning under singular circumstances. She was employed as a servant at Kearsley Road, Highfield, and, when called by her mistress at seven o'clock, she answered as usual. She went downstairs soon after and was heard going about her duties of preparing breakfast. At eight o'clock her mistress went into the kitchen and was horrified to see the girl hanging by a rope from a hook on the ceiling. The body was cut down and, although it was still warm, the girl was dead. She had taken a piece of old clothes line and had attached one end to the hook and the other she had wrapped several times around her neck, and then she appeared to have thrown herself off a chair. She must have been strangled by her own body weight as her feet touched the ground. Her mistress could not give any account as to why she should do this dreadful deed. (*Sheffield Journal*)

JUNE 18TH

1832: Great celebrations at the news of the passing of the Reform Bill and the enfranchisement of Sheffield were seen today. In anticipation of the events, people had been busy decorating carriages and carts to use in the procession. From early in the morning, 3,000 people with flags assembled on the Wicker. These were then joined by 5,000 people belonging to the Political Union, each bearing a medal struck especially for the occasion. The procession of decorated carriages crossed over Lady Bridge, followed by the decorated carriage of the Printers Union. Their display exhibited presses at work, as well as other various trades, the various displays followed for a length of two miles. The procession, after taking a circuit of the town, assembled on the New Market in the afternoon, where a hollow square was formed by the people. A hymn was sung which had been written by Sheffield poet, Ebenezer Elliott. The great body of the assembled people then retired to numerous houses, where there was little doubt that the celebrations would continue. Fifteen hundred of the principal men of the town, with local MP Mr T.A. Ward at their head, proceeded to partake of a public dinner at Hyde Park. (Leader, R.E., *Sheffield in the Eighteenth Century*, Sheffield, Sir W.C. Leng & Co., 1905)

JUNE 19TH

1863: A report on a fire which had taken place at the Exchange Brewery belonging to Messrs Tennant Bros in Bridge Street was published in today's newspapers. In the centre of the extensive premises was a lofty tower, the upper part of which was occupied by the malting rooms, the mashing apparatus etc. It seems that the fire broke out at 8 a.m. in the malting room and made considerable progress before it was discovered. Information was given to the police and the fire engines attended with promptness, although it was some time before water could be obtained, as the mains were off at that time. The police and the firemen were obliged to get onto the roof of the lower building in order to tackle the fire in the tower. After two hours the fire was finally extinguished. The roof of the tower was almost entirely destroyed and considerable damage was done to the upper storeys and to the mashing machinery. The total damage was estimated to be between £400 and £500. The greatest loss, however, was felt by the enforced suspension of operations during the repairs to the building. The well-directed energy of the police and the fire brigade deserved great commendation. (*Sheffield Times*)

JUNE 20TH

1831: Sheffield suffered the worst outbreak of illness it had seen in a number of years. However, it was by no means of an alarming nature. Not cholera, nor typhus fever, nor any of those pestilential diseases from which Sheffield has fallen victim in the past; the epidemic was, for the most part, of a very mild character, a kind of catarrhal fever, presenting at its onset the usual symptoms of common influenza. With little care and proper treatment, the ailment was relieved within the course of two or three days. The origins of this affection were attributed to the unexpectedly cold weather, which had begun ten or so days prior to the outbreak. Nevertheless, the epidemic resulted in a loss of work for many of the town's manufacturers. (*Sheffield Courant*)

JUNE 21ST

1820: On this day a meeting of the town trustees was held for the purpose of celebrating the King's Coronation (George IV) on August 1st next. The meeting, which was held in the Town Hall, held many of the principle gentlemen of the town. The meeting selected a committee who would be in charge of the festivities. The town trustees were anxious to show proper respect to the King from the people of Sheffield. It was quickly resolved that 'this Trust subscribe the sum of 15 guineas towards a public exhibition of fireworks on the above occasion'. A further sum of £4 5s (making altogether £20) was also offered 'to defray the expenses of firing the great guns'. It was also resolved that a sum not exceeding 25 guineas 'shall be also subscribed by the town trustees towards the expenses of providing fifty coats and hats to be given to that number of poor men of the same age of the King or upwards. These men will then walk in a procession on the day of the celebration. This is on the proviso that the Cutler's Company and the Church Burgesses agree to subscribe each, the same sum out of their funds, for the above purpose.' (Leader, J.D., *The Records of the Burgery of Sheffield*, Sheffield Independent Press, 1897)

JUNE 22ND

1847: On this day, regrettably, there occurred the suicide of Inspector Thomas Wakefield, who, for the eight years prior to the incident, had been a member of the Sheffield police force. It appeared that he had suffered domestic differences with his wife in consequence of her intemperate habits. He had frequently stated to his fellow officers that he wished either she or he were dead. He said just recently that she had sold almost every item of clothing and pieces of furniture to buy drink. He showed one of the officers a pistol a short while ago, saying that 'he would never be seen alive again'. During the afternoon of the previous day, whilst his wife was at a neighbouring dram shop on the Wicker, he barricaded the door at 5 p.m. and went upstairs. Shortly afterwards, the sound of a pistol shot was heard. PC North was on duty, hearing the shot, broke down the door. In the attic was the unfortunate man; he was dead. In his pocket, a scrap of paper was found with his last words: 'No human being knows what a miserable three months I have passed. T.W.' The inquest was to be held on the death later on in the day. (*Sheffield Times*)

JUNE 23RD

1844: A report regarding the colliers of the town, who were still on strike, was printed today, although it was noted that the men and their families were suffering severely. The reporter stated that: 'We have seen a requisition to the Mayor to call a public meeting to complain of the inconvenience arising from the want of coal, and to endeavour to bring around an arrangement between the masters and the men. For ourselves, we do not see any prospect of advantage arising in such a matter. A public meeting cannot enter fully into the question at issue; it cannot call the parties to plead their case, nor should it judge either party unheard. We beg earnestly that the strike be settled soon and the men and boys returned to work.' Yesterday, a large crowd had collected in Fargate to witness the conveyance of a wagon load of bread from the Old Green Dragon to the Robin Hood public house in the Park. The bread was given as a present from the table knife forgers to the starving colliers. The wagon, containing 600 loaves, was pulled through the streets by men and boys. (*Sheffield Independent*)

JUNE 24TH

1850: An inquest was held on the death of a woman called Mary Warrener (50) today at the Acorn Inn, Shalesmoor. She was reported as being 'an immoral woman' who lived with a man called Frederick Allott, who had several times assaulted her. Neighbours were used to hearing her screams, although she denied his ill-treatment of her. She became ill on June 9th, but no steps were taken to obtain medical assistance until June 12th, when surgeon Mr N. Moore was called in. He found her to be suffering from an attack of palsy, which had affected her speech. Whilst in the room where the woman lay, Mr Moore spotted that some stains on the wall, resembling blood, had been covered up by a coat of whitewash. Mary's daughter told him that the house was riddled with a loathsome vermin. The coroner asked that a post-mortem be carried out on the dead woman's body, but the causes were not obvious and a verdict of accidental death was recorded. The coroner requested that the bedding be burnt and the Sanitary Committee be informed of the state of the house. (*Sheffield Independent*)

JUNE 25TH

1844: It was announced in the *Sheffield Iris* today that the River Dun Company were starting upon a programme of improvements to the rivers and canals of Sheffield. The reporter stated that: 'We are glad to inform our readers that the River Dun Company have commenced their promised alteration and improvements in the river between this town and Stainforth. They are now erecting swing bridges over the canal, and are likewise deepening the river, so as to make good navigation for vessels 150 tons burthen, which is about double the extent of the present navigation. There is, we believe, little doubt that the intention is ultimately to make a still water navigation to this town, a step which will be of the greatest benefit to the inhabitants generally, and will tend greatly to increase the importance of the borough. We understand it is also intended that there shall be direct communication between Doncaster and Hull by means of steam packets'. The work, which was to commence straight away, was hoped to be finished in two years time and the benefit to Sheffield enormous. The canal and the river traffic would later be appreciated by the many manufacturers who were able to transport their goods by water. (*Sheffield Iris*)

JUNE 26TH

1668: On this night a man named John Bowman, a tailor, was travelling from Sheffield market towards Heeley and was about midway when he was overtaken by another man named John Broomhead. The two men travelled together until they came to the Cutler's Bridge, where they discussed the apparition which had lately been seen upon the bridge. The apparition took the form of a man known as Earle George. As they were discussing the apparition, there suddenly appeared to them a man dressed like a prince in a green doublet and ruff and holding a brachete (a kind of hound) in his hands. Not surprisingly, John Bowman was described as being 'sorely affrighted and fell into a swoon or a trance and continued in the same as he concieveth for the space of about half an hour'. When he finally awoke, he found himself on the road alone. Then he saw a man with two loaded packhorses and travelled with him the rest of the way. He later made this statement and swore this was true in front of the magistrate Francis Barker Esq., which was copied by town clerk Mr Thomas Raine. (*Raine Deposition from York Castle*)

JUNE 27TH

1852: The 37th anniversary of the Battle of Waterloo was held on this day at the Greyhound Inn, Gibraltar Street, and was attended by thirty veterans of the battlefield. They met to commemorate the anniversary and the show of order was kept by the beating of a drum and the notes of a fife, which assembled the group. Most of them wore medals on their breasts, and some even three, tokens of their service in the Peninsula and of the battles they had fought. The table was loaded with a large saddle of roast beef of excellent quality – a favourite of the English. At the conclusion of the dinner, and after a brief interval, the usual loyal military and other appropriate toasts were given by the chairman, Mr Deakin, and several others. At 5.30 p.m., the wives of the veterans, twenty-five in number according to arrangements, met in another room to take tea together, during which time the drum and fife kept playing, and the evening was spent in singing and dancing until 10 p.m., when the final toast was given by the chair and the company separated. (*Sheffield Free Press*)

JUNE 28TH

1872: A curious case was heard at Sheffield Town Hall today when an application for a summons for conspiracy had been made against Ebenezer Richardson and Sarah Gamble. A person named Mrs Sarah Whitaker, living in Bailey Street, had a twenty-two-year-old son by a former husband, who was weak in intellect. The parents had worked hard with him in order that he could make a living for himself as a scissor setter. In financial matters he was helpless as his mother had to take him to the bank for any transactions, but nevertheless he had managed to save a total of £12. A man named Richardson told him that he had to get married and introduced him to his sister-in-law, Sarah Gamble. He also told him that he had to get the money out of his bank account without his mother finding out, so that he would be able to buy furniture for the marital home. The next day his mother found out about the proposed marriage and put a stop to it, but Richardson and Gamble refused to give up the furniture. The case was adjourned to the following week. On Monday 8th July the magistrate found no case of fraud and dismissed the case. (*Sheffield Independent*)

JUNE 29TH

1831: Today, the ladies belonging to the congregation of St Phillips' Church presented to the excellent minister a most superb silver epergne weighing upwards of 100 ounces, manufactured by Messrs C.F. Younge of the High Street, Sheffield. The reporter stated that 'We have the opportunity of inspecting this valuable present and can bear testimony to the novelty and elegance of the design and the richness and perfection of the workmanship'. A set of glasses which accompany was also presented by the ladies of the congregation. On the foot of these articles were engraved the armorial bearings of the reverend gentleman and the following suitable inscription: 'Presented by the Ladies of the Congregation of St Phillip's Church, Sheffield to the Revd Thomas Dinham Atkinson MA, June 24th 1831 as a memorial of their high regard of him and their sincere regret at losing so zealous and affectionate a Minister.' The epergne was deposited in a very neat mahogany case prepared for the purpose. The paper reported that 'our own knowledge of Mr Atkinson's character inclines us to a hearty approval of this tribute, and we are sure it must be as peculiarly gratifying to the receiver as it undoubtedly is to the givers.' (*Sheffield Courant*)

JUNE 30TH

1903: The city of Sheffield was visited today by the Lord Mayor of London, Sir Marcus Samuel, in order to lay the foundation stone of the new University College, to be erected at the cost of £100,000. He was received at the station by the Duke of Norfolk, the Lord Mayor of Sheffield, as well as other councillors and officials. The celebrations started when Sir Marcus was presented with the Freedom of the City at the Town Hall, and the procession then went up to the site of the new college. The route was lined by a crowd of spectators, who cheered heartily. The procession was led by mounted Yeomanry and followed by a detachment of Volunteers. Alderman Franklin, who was the honorary treasurer to the college, stated that: 'Sheffield University College was first established as Firth College in 1879 and now consists of the University College, the Sheffield Medical School founded in 1828, and the Technical School in 1883. New buildings were now being erected for the metallurgical department which promises to become the most efficient and well-equipped institutions of its time.' Sir Marcus laid the foundation stone and was later given a dinner at the Cutler's Hall. (*The Times*)

JULY 1ST

1842: The Cutler's Company received a reply to the telegram they they had sent to Her Majesty Queen Victoria, Prince Albert and the Duchess of Kent, on the occasion of the attempt of treason against the Queen's life. The reply to Mr Thomas Ellin junior, the Master Cutler, read:

Buckingham Palace June 17th 1842

Sir,

I am commanded by his Royal Highness Prince Albert to acknowledge and thank the Master, Wardens, Searchers, Assistants and the Corporation of Cutlers of Sheffield for their Address and Congratulations on the recent providential escape of her Most Gracious Majesty the Queen.

There was even a reply from the Duchess of Kent which read:

Clarence House June 18th 1842

Sir,

Having had the honour to place before Her Royal Highness the address of the Master, Wardens, Searchers, Assistants of the Corporation of Cutler at Sheffield on the merciful preservation of the Queen from the treasonable attempt against Her Majesty. I am charged by Her Royal Highness to express Her Royal Highnesses' grateful acknowledgement of their sympathy on an event so foreign to the character of the British People.

(Hey, D., *A History of Sheffield*, Carnegie Publishing Ltd, 1998)

JULY 2ND

1842: It was announced in the *Sheffield Independent* today that a School of Design was to be established in Sheffield. A petition was at the time being collected for the Board of Trade requesting that the city may participate in the government grant made for that purpose. It was also reported that the Cutler's Company and the town trustee have both promised 'very liberal' annual subscriptions towards its maintenance as well as some bankers, chief merchants and manufacturers. The *Independent* stated that: 'It would be a reproach upon "classic Sheffield" were she not to bestir herself on this subject. Of the great utility of such an institution there can scarcely be two opinions and we hope soon to see our young artists employing their pencils on works of the most eminent ancient and modern masters, whose chisels have won for them a reputation and a name as lasting as the marble on which they were employed.' A letter written by 'Carolus' was inserted in the same newspaper, stating that, 'I have had many fears that this noble project would miscarry so far as Sheffield was concerned, but I think it is now fairly launched.' The Sheffield School of Art was founded in 1843. (*Sheffield Independent*)

July 3rd

1826: It was reported today that requests for subscriptions to help the poor and needy of the town had fallen short, leaving the townspeople suffering from impoverished markets and industrial distress. Among the unemployed were several tradespersons. A committee has been appointed, requesting food or labour for these people. The workhouse authorities have issued tickets for flour, oatmeal and bread last week, which exceeded £135. Over fifty able-bodied and willing-minded unemployed cutlers were engaged in tidying up the burial grounds of St George's Church. Upwards of a hundred more offered themselves for similar labour on the site of the intended church (St Mary's) on Bramall Lane. The committee applied to Earl Fitzwilliam and today they received a response to Revd Thomas Sutton:

Milton 29th June 1826

Dear Sir,
I send enclosed a bill for £200 as my mite towards the relief of the artisans of Sheffield. What I owe to them can never be out of my recollection and will ever bring to my mind the debt of gratitude which I owe to them in so eminent a degree.

Such generosity from the 'never failing friend' was exceptional, as he had recently donated £500 to a similar cause in London. (*Sheffield Iris*)

JULY 4TH

1844: A serious disturbance at Soap House Pit of the Sheffield Coal Company took place today. Eighteen men arrived at Sheffield station to work in the pit at about 8.15 a.m. Aware that there might be repercussions from striking miners, the men were accompanied on their journey by police. As they entered the yard, the miners booed the men and called them 'knobsticks'. By 9.15 a.m., a crowd of people arrived and began throwing stones at the premises. Some of the men gained entrance into the yard and broke open the gates. At this time, the chief constable, who had only four men with him, sent for reinforcements and he took refuge at the Tontine Inn. The crowd had broken open the door of the premises and attacked the miners with sticks and anything to hand and the militia was called out. Ten of the miners were rescued and taken to the Town Hall. A troop of Lancers, followed in a very short time by two companies of the 70th Foot, set about dispersing the crowd. The following day, eight of the men returned to the colliery and those who had been injured were cared for at the Rose and Crown on Waingate. (*Sheffield Independent*)

JULY 5TH

1854: Today's newspapers carried a report about the number of carters being brought before the magistrates. They were charged with obstruction by leaving their carts in the streets, particularly on the open space around the pump in West Bar. The case had previously been brought before the Bench, and had been adjourned in order that Mr Clark Branson, who was defending the carters, could send a memorial to the Watch Committee, who had the power to grant the land for the use of carters. The Mayor said that a 'very respectfully signed memorial was presented to the Watch Committee at their meeting on Thursday evening', which he attended. However, the committee declined to interfere and left the matter in the hands of the magistrates. The fact was, the traffic into the town had increased so much that the leaving of the carts caused serious obstructions, and complaints had constantly been made about them. Chief constable, Mr Raynor, was urged to ensure that something was done about the obstruction. Mr Branson stated that his clients could not deny the offence, but had acted under what they thought was a right; they should not be fined on this occasion. The defendants consented to pay the costs of the summons. (*Sheffield Free Press*)

JULY 6TH

1857: *Sheffield Times* today printed the cases that were due to be tried at the assizes at York. It stated that: 'The civil business from the neighbourhood of Sheffield is unusually meagre for the Summer Assize court this month. Notices had been given for the trial of a breach of promise case, between Miss Dudson and Mr Lawton, but the defendant, a clerk in the office of Mr Isaac Ironside, an accountant, has allowed the judgement to go by default. As a result of this, it leaves only the damages to be assessed to Miss Dudson before the Sheriff. The only other case of interest we have heard of is an unfortunate action brought by Mrs Middleton, a widow living in Netherthorpe Street, for damages for the seduction of her daughter. The defendant is a person named Wheatcroft, who was formerly a butcher and baker in the same neighbourhood. It seems that he gave up his business, and was on the point of leaving the country just before the last assize (at which the action was expected to be tried). Fortunately, he was arrested on an absconding debtors warrant and confined at York Castle debtors' prison.' (*Sheffield Times*)

July 7th

1883: A report of an extraordinary carriage accident in Heeley on Saturday afternoon appeared in the local papers today. After a lovely day out, a 'pleasure party' was being driven in an open, three-wheeled carriage through Heeley in the direction of Sheffield. When they reached the bottom of Well Road, the carriage suddenly swerved and hit the back part of a tramcar. The jolting of the carriage caused the horse to bolt, and the driver lost all control over it. The passengers began screaming, which frightened the horse even more. The demented animal rushed along Heeley Road, dragging the carriage and its several occupants in 'a very undesirable fashion'. The carriage went down Queens Road and dashed past a man who tried to stop it, near to the Surrey Hotel. Continuing its career along Queens Road, it passed the lamp at the junction of St Mary's Road and then dashed up Shrewsbury Road. There the sudden rise in the ground brought the horse to a standstill and it was immediately secured by the driver. The occupants of the carriage alighted, dazedly sound of limb, having been greatly frightened after their somewhat perilous journey in a conveyance drawn by a runaway horse. (*Daily Telegraph*)

JULY 8TH

1867: Trade unions in Sheffield had been accused of using murder and arson to intimidate non-union workers, and a Trade Commission had been appointed to look into these crimes. On this day there was a large meeting of working men convened by Revd R. Stainton in Paradise Square, where he made the following speech: 'That this meeting of the thousands of working men of Sheffield declare that it views with the deepest shame and abhorrence the systematic crimes which have disgraced the trades of the town and that the foul deeds and those that have committed them are enemies to working men in general and to trade unions in particular. This meeting also expresses its thanks to the Government for the course it adopted for the detection of the criminals, and its high admiration in the way in which they have prosecuted their work. We as working men and citizens of Sheffield, venture to hope that from this time, a better state of things may exist amongst us. We declare our readiness and determination to do all in our power to redeem the character of our town whereby some of its inhabitants has been brought under such bitter reproach.' (Leader, R.E., *Sheffield in the Eighteenth Century*, Sheffield, Sir W.C. Leng & Co., 1905)

July 9th

1863: It was reported that three men had been apprehended and taken before the magistrate yesterday, charged with the jewel robbery of a shop owned by Mr Myers on 12 March last. Two men, who had been captured in Sheffield, were taken before the magistrates at noon. The men, Martin Cooper of Milton Street and William James Sykes of Rockingham Street, were found to have some of the stolen watches still in their possession. The men were remanded in charge and, later that day, Detective Inspector Airey arrived from Liverpool, where he had arrested the third member of the gang, John Walker of Rotherham. Cooper was thought to be the instigator behind the robbery, as he had been in the employ of Mr Myers at the time of the theft. A larger amount of stolen goods have been seized in London, which had been identified by Mr Myers as being his property. The reporter stated that: 'We were led to believe that the police have a very good case against the three men who will no doubt be sent to the assizes'. The men were tried at York Assizes in December 1863 and each was sentenced to eighteen months' imprisonment in Wakefield Prison. (*Sheffield Times*)

July 10th

1840: An account of a fearful accident which happened yesterday in Blind Lane appeared in today's newspapers. 'At the end of the lane, nearest to West Street, some property has about a fortnight ago become untenanted for the purpose of being pulled down to widen the street. A number of boys, having been amusing themselves for several evenings past, anticipated the labourers' work by smashing windows, destroying roofs, pulling down walls, and so on. During the onslaught of this destruction, a part of the gable end fell down upon them, and for a time it was believed that some were killed. As the rumours flew around the town that several boys had been killed, people flocked to the scene and help was at hand and several men began to dig through the rubble. Thankfully the boys' voices could be heard shouting, and they were one after the other extricated from the rubble. Five boys in all were carried down to Messrs Overend and Russell's surgery, where it was ascertained that only boy had been seriously hurt. His leg was broken in two places, but it was quite clear that he would make a full recovery. Perhaps this would have taught a lesson to other children tempted to play in ruins.' (*Sheffield Mercury*)

JULY 11TH

1872: On this night, a massive thunderstorm over Sheffield caused much damage to every street in the city, but, thankfully, with no loss of life. The usual means of carrying away surplus water was completely insufficient, and hundreds of cellars were flooded, the water being in some of them 4 to 5ft deep. The Don and the Sheaf were soon deluged and their banks submerged. People collected on Lady Bridge to watch the waters gushing beneath them. Heavy surface water ran down Waingate and pavement stones were torn up in the torrent. Cellars were flooded in West Bar and all the streets surrounding the area and South Street were completely impassable. Public houses throughout the city complained that, with the cellars flooded, bungs had come out of several beer barrels and their contents mingled with the flood. A grocer found that his flooded cellar resulted in the loss of a huge amount of butter, hams, cheese and bacon. Householders found water in the houses up to the 'second bar of the fire grate', as one lady put it. Drains could not hold all the water, which further added to the problem. (*Sheffield Times*)

July 12th

1839: Today was printed an advertisement of the appointment of Messrs Wilkinson & Co., manufacturers of scissors to the Queen. It was described that the scissors presented to Her Majesty were of a most splendid specimen of workmanship. On the shanks of the scissor were displayed in beautiful etching the Royal Coat of Arms ornamented by exquisite scroll work. On the one bow were the words '*Honi Soit qui mal y pense*' (Shamed be he who thinks evil of it) on the other '*Dieu et mon droit*' (God and My Right – which was the motto of the British Monarch). The letter in reply to Mr Wilkinson stated:

Windsor Castle, June 14th 1839

Sir Henry Wheatley begs to acknowledge the receipt of Mr Wilkinson's letter, and the case containing a pair of scissors, which he has not failed to submit to the Queen; and Sir Henry is directed to express Her Majesty's admiration of the workmanship and execution, which reflects much credit on those such employed. The scissors Her Majesty is pleased to retain, I remain Sir, Your obliged servant

An advertisement in another part of the same newspaper reflects the pride in which Messrs Wilkinson & Co. announce themselves as 'Scissor Manufacturer to Queen Victoria.' (*Daily Telegraph*)

July 13th

1864: At a Town Council meeting held today, the Watch Committee presented a letter which had been received from Her Majesty's Inspector of Police, Lt General J. Woodford, regarding the state of the cells at the Town Hall. It was suggested that 'by reason of their position and excessive dampness they must be injurious to the health of the prisoners'. He warned that he had complained two years previously about the same thing and, as nothing had been accomplished, he was compelled to pass on his findings to the Secretary of State, unless it was decided that the use of the cells will cease. The chief constable of Sheffield, Mr Jackson, stated that due to overcrowding, some of the cells had to be used that were not fit for 'any living things except for the reptiles that crawled on the walls'. It seems that the Watch Committee had been in negotiations with the town trustees to either buy another property, in which to have new cells built, or to build an extension to the present Town Hall. It was finally agreed, after a lot of discussion, that the letter would be passed onto the chairman of the new Town Hall Committee, Alderman Mycock, for his views. *Sheffield Independent*)

JULY 14TH

1874: It was announced that there had been a vast increase in the price of coal, as a result of the coal miner's strike. The reporter of the *Sheffield Post* stated that: 'One of the results of the colliery strike has been to send up the price of coal by almost a third, to what it was before the strike. We hear that these largely increased prices were asked yesterday by many of the coal merchants and coal owners. This has led to the posting of notices in some of the principle manufacturing establishments of Sheffield informing the workmen that, in the event of coal going up in value and becoming scarce, the different manufacturing works will be closed until fuel can be obtained at a price which prevailed before the strike. It will thus be seen that the dispute now going on between the coal owners and their miners, will need to be settled without delay, otherwise, this strike will have a more prejudicial effect on large numbers of workmen, who have neither directly nor indirectly had anything to do with it. We urge that some kind of agreement be come to as quickly as possible in order for this dilemma to be resolved.' (*Sheffield Post*)

JULY 15TH

1895: A fire in Gilpin Street in a house occupied by Mrs Sarah Gyte was reported today. Mrs Gyte had been storing clothing of all descriptions, which had been given to her by people for whom she had worked for over forty years. On July 14th, she left home and locked up her house as usual, and, soon after, a neighbour's chimney caught fire. During the day, smoke was seen issuing from the chimney of Mrs Gyte's dwelling, but it was not until late in the afternoon that the house was seen to be on fire. Notice was given to the Longsett Road police, and Inspector Goodwin was soon at the scene. The fire brigade was telephoned at 4.24 p.m. and in ten minutes they were at the scene of the fire. Breaking into the house, they found that the bedroom and garret were on fire, and the staircase was almost burnt away, and the ceilings of both rooms were also burning. The flames were soon extinguished, but both rooms and the staircase were considerably damaged. It was thought that the blaze was caused by a spark from the neighbour's chimney falling down Mrs Gyte's chimney and setting fire to the clothes stored in the house. (*Daily Telegraph*)

JULY 16TH

1857: For several nights of the previous week, and for part of this week, 'Dr Mark and His Little Men' gave vocal and instrumental concerts in the Music Hall. The reporter for the *Sheffield Free Press* stated that 'his talented little men' numbering almost forty, were made up of extremely young lads, who played on wind, string and other instruments. The 'entertainment is of a varied character consisting of cornet and other solos, songs, fantasias and operatic selections. The performances generally are such as to elicit the most cordial applause from the audience. The precision and effect from which the boys play in full chorus is wonderful, considering their extreme youth, and their solos are no less admirably given and are frequently encored. In the "laughing chorus" the little men are particularly amusing from the great zest with which they entered into the piece. The entertainment is a novel one and is a striking illustration of the efficiency of Dr Mark's training, and the capabilities of children to understand and render music.' Encouraging the people of Sheffield to make sure they did not miss this unique entertainment, the reporter urged them 'to find an opportunity to attend – they may rely upon having a treat'. (*Sheffield Free Press*)

JULY 17TH

1854: This afternoon an inquest was held at the Hillsborough Inn, before Mr T. Badger, the coroner, on the death of Joseph Crookes of Owlerton. He had died following a number a serious injuries sustained in an attack made on him by a party of men on the morning of July 4th. The deceased had been to the Owlerton Feast, during which he had danced with a number of people and it was reported that he was quite merry. Suddenly, one of the men in his party began to quarrel with him and he challenged Crookes to a fight. The matter was settled for the time being, and the party went to the house of an acquaintance and continued drinking. When Crookes left the house at about 2 a.m., he had hardly got through the door before he was knocked senseless by men brandishing pieces of wood, and it was from those effects that he died. The jury felt it their painful duty, after considerable discussion, to return a verdict of willful murder against John Holroyd, George Knowles, Charles Haines, George Tomlinson and Joseph Peach. Holroyd and Peach were then removed to Wakefield prison. Warrants for Knowles, Haines and Tomlinson were issued, as they were still at large. (*Sheffield Examiner*)

JULY 18TH

1873: A report on Mr Wright's Patent Air Gas, which was demonstrated by lighting the premises of Mr Cooper on West Bar, was reported today. 'The apparatus for the manufacture of the gas is put down on the adjoining premises. It consists of an ometer, from which the air is forced into a cylinder, the chambers of which contain charcoal alternated with layers of cotton, steeped with carbonized petroleum. The air that leaves the cylinder is inflammable gas. It can be produced at half the price of ordinary coal gas. Mr Cooper's premises contained 130 burners and they were lit last night, for the first time, with the air gas. The opinion of Mr Cooper and other shopkeepers of West Bar was that the light was superior to that produced by the old gas. Mr Wright has a smaller apparatus which he is presently working on which, to silversmith's braziers and persons using a blow pipe, will be invaluable. Mr Cooper maintained that the gas will be most useful for the lighting up of omnibuses, trains, vessels and so forth. It was thought that such a discovery at the present time was of great importance.' (*Sheffield Times*)

JULY 19TH

1819: A sense of great alarm in the town was rife, due to a number of deaths caused by bites from rabies-ridden dogs. A public meeting was held and orders signed by the magistrates for the destruction of all dogs found in the streets. £700 was subscribed for expenses and defence of actions brought by the owners of the said dogs. (Leader, R., *Sheffield Local Directory*, Sheffield Independent Press, 1830)

———◆———

1850: Terrible thunderstorms visited Sheffield and its neighbourhood today. 'The rain descended in torrents while flash after flash of forked lightning followed each other in quick succession'. It seems that a house on Pomona Street, Ecclesall was struck by 'electric fluid' which descended into the sitting room, where a visitor was knocked down but not injured. The Wesleyan chapel at Ecclesfield was struck on the south east gable. The lightning, after tearing away part of the roof, passed into the chapel over the end gallery. The pews in this gallery, as a result, 'are much broken and the strong oak bearers shiver like matchsticks'. Two cottages at Ragg Wheel were damaged, the lightning knocking down part of a chimney stack and passing into the bedrooms of the two houses. (*Sheffield Courant*)

July 20th

1840: A woman named Mrs Moorwood appeared at the Sheffield police court today to show just cause why she should not pay for the maintenance of her grandchildren, at present in the workhouse. Her son, who was described as 'a dissolute young man', had abandoned his offspring years ago, leaving them chargeable to the parish. The solicitor for the workhouse stated the facts of the case and contended that under the new Poor Law Amendment Act, in the absence of the children's parents, the grandfather or grandmother were answerable for the support of their grandchildren. Mrs Moorwood was proved to have an estate of more than £400 a year, and therefore could afford to make such payments. For the defence, it was enforced that the magistrates had powers given them under the Act, which merely stated that the offspring were obliged to support the ascending branch, making no provision at all for a case like this. The father could not be said to come within the meaning of the words of the Act; as an impotent, old or disabled person. The magistrates, after consulting together, decided in favour of the workhouse authorities and made an order on Mrs Moorwood for 4s and 6d per week. (*Sheffield Iris*)

JULY 21ST

1885: A report on a boiler explosion, submitted by Mr Peter Samson, who held an enquiry on behalf of the Board of Trade, was published today. The premises on Eldon Street were owned by Mr John Vardy, a blacksmith. The cause of the explosion the previous April was caused by the collapse and consequent rupture of the fire box. It was examined and found to be too weak to sustain with safety the ordinary working pressure. The plates were all pitted over the inner surface and were uniformly thin by corrosion on the fireside. The boiler was not insured, nor was it regularly inspected, as Mr Vardy maintained it himself. His inspection involved merely looking at the fire box through the firing hole, and therefore he did not see the defects. Mr Samson said 'the corrosion on the fire side of the firebox plates were of a uniform character, frequently observed in boilers that were not in constant use. Such corrosion is very deceptive to persons not skilled in boiler inspection, and it is not surprising that Mr Vardy did not observe it when looking through the firing hole'. Mr Samson concluded that a person qualified to examine such boilers would readily have detected the defect. (*Daily Telegraph*)

JULY 22ND

1829: On this day the venerable Earl Fitzwilliam, accompanied by the surgeon Mr Pierce, arrived at Sheffield, from his estate at Wentworth House. It was gratifying to the Sheffield people to see that he had recovered from his recent illness. Indeed his life was thought to be near to its close, and his son, Lord Milton, was sent for from London to be with his father. The eighty-two-year-old Earl walked from the Tontine Inn to view the new market houses he had lately caused to be erected on Sheffield Moor. He was accompanied by his son and several others, thought to be ladies and gentlemen who had been visiting the estate during the Earl's indisposition. Although the Earl appeared to be considerably reduced, with the help of Mr Pierce on one hand, and a stick on the other, he managed to hold himself erect. Earl Fitzwilliam had long been held high in the affections of the people of Sheffield for the many acts of kindness he had shown to the people of the town. As he climbed into the coach to leave, which took him back to Wentworth, he was given a great cheer. (*Sheffield Courant*)

JULY 23RD

1791: The Enclosure Act was brought to Sheffield between the years of 1788 and 1795. Fierce opposition was shown to these enclosures, when it was announced that the Crookesmoor racecourse would have to be closed. On this day, the Revd James Wilkinson (vicar and magistrate), Mr Joseph Ward (Master Cutler), and Mr Vincent Eyre (agent to the Duke of Norfolk) had all requested military aid to allow the work to go ahead. They claimed that 'considerable bodies of disorderly people in this neighbourhood have lately, several times, assembled in considerable force, with the riotous intention of preventing the Commissioners acting under the authority of the Enclosure Bill... Not only have they driven them from the commons, but also menaced them with the greatest personal danger if they attempted to proceed with the enclosures. These disorderly mobs have actually burned farm property, and broke the windows of several houses. They have menaced the lives and property of the freeholders enclosure and openly avowed their intention of laying open the enclosures in the neighbourhood already made... They have also burned the houses of all the freeholders who have countenanced the late enclosures'. (Hey, D., *A History of Sheffield*, Carnegie Publishers Ltd, 1998)

JULY 24TH

1870: It was announced today that the American consulate for Sheffield, Mr G.J. Abbott, was to be recalled back to the United States. It seems that the American government was acting on a policy of regularly changing its representatives in Europe. Mr Abbott was appointed in the spring of 1863, as the United States consulate in Sheffield. He was the last official appointed under the former administration to be withdrawn from his post on this side of the Atlantic. 'It is true that the unfortunate circumstances of the late dispute on the question of invoicing steel, have to some extent brought Mr Abbot into collision with some of our local manufacturers. The question raised touched steel makers in so tender a point, which it was quite impossible for anyone standing in the delicate position Mr Abbott occupied, towards both sides, to avoid incurring unpopularity. But it is perhaps not too much to say that few could have performed an unpleasant task with more tact and courtesy.' (*Sheffield Independent*)

JULY 25TH

1899: A number of newspapers on this day announced that Sheffield had taken delivery of fifty new electric trams from Messrs George F. Milnes and Co. of Birkenhead. Thirty-eight were double-deckers, and twelve were single deck trams, the former having a seating capacity of fifty-one passengers and the latter a capacity of twenty-eight. The electric motors were out of sight under the body of the tram, and the only visible piece of equipment was the trolley bar, conducting the electric current from the overhead wires to the car. The interior of the trams were fitted with oak and ash, and the seats were provided with cushions, upholstered with crimson Utrecht velvet. The seat backs were of a lath and space construction of contrasting woods, nicely curved for comfort. Messrs Milnes also had under construction two sample composite trams, each with three compartments, the two end ones being for the use of smokers and the centre one for non-smokers. Each of these trams were to carry twenty-eight passengers, sixteen in the centre and six each in the end compartments. The smoking compartments on one of the trams were fitted with sliding windows, whilst on the other tram they were left entirely open with an ornamental, wrought iron grill. (Leader, R., *Sheffield Local Directory*, Sheffield Independent Press, 1830)

JULY 26TH

1861: An announcement that the Montgomery Monument would be unveiled the following Monday featured in the newspapers on this day. The poet, Mr James Montgomery, died on April 10th 1854 and he received a magnificent public funeral in Sheffield on May 11th. On the 24th of that month, a meeting was held at which it was resolved to erect a monument. It was decided that the eminent sculptor John Bell Esq. should be employed to execute the monument, and it should be erected over the grave of the poet. Mr Bell was invited to Sheffield and, having examined the proposed site, he undertook to prepare a model, which, the following September, was exhibited at the Cutler's Hall. It was judged to be a beautiful piece of high artistic merit and would cost £3,500. On May 4th, a committee was elected to start a subscription but nothing was done for two years, until the Sheffield Sunday School Union stated that they themselves proposed to erect their own monument. In July 1856, only part of the cost had been raised, and Mr Bell was approached to make a cheaper version made out of bronze. It stands upon a square granite pedestal, on two faces of which there is an inscription to the great man. (*Sheffield Times*)

JULY 27TH

1791: On this day a troop of Light Dragoons arrived in the town from Nottingham to quell the disturbances caused by the Enclosure Act (*see* July 23rd). Excited by their arrival, a large crowd gathered in the town centre. About 9 p.m., a mob of several hundred people attacked the nearest symbol of authority, the town gaol in King Street, breaking its windows and freeing the prisoners. The shout then went up 'To Broom Hall' (the home of Vicar Wilkinson, the town's only magistrate). The mob broke all his windows, smashed parts of his furniture, damaged and burned his library and set his haystacks on fire, before being dispersed by the Dragoons. Back in town, they broke the windows of the Duke of Norfolk's agent, Vincent Eyre. The following day more soldiers arrived from York and order was restored. Five rioters, who had been arrested, were examined a few days later at the Tontine Inn by Col. Althorpe of Dinnington Hall and committed to York Assizes. Four of them were subsequently released but John Bennet was found guilty of arson and hanged on 7 September. The town trustees paid £561 expenses in compensation to the victims of the riot. Sheffield had never witnessed anything as serious before. (Hey, D., *A History of Sheffield,* Carnegie Publishing Ltd, 1998)

July 28th

1825: A highly respectable meeting took place in Sheffield, at which it was resolved to adopt more efficient measures for checking the violation of the Sabbath. The report published today said that the town and its neighbourhood had been divided into districts, in each of which Special Constables have been appointed, for the express purpose of preserving order in their respective neighbourhoods on Sundays. Not one of these constables was expected to be on duty above once a month. The chair of the meeting said that: 'Very little exertion had been requisite to carry into effect this judicious arrangement, which had fully answered the intentions of the benevolent persons who originated it'. The many parks and amusement grounds around the town were now open to the public, but it was expected that some exertion would be required to prevent violent scenes. He pointed out that: 'If Sunday be not constituted to the best day of the week, it almost unnecessarily becomes the worst. From the platform of the gallows, thousands of bitter, but voluntary, confessions have been made that early abuse of the Sabbath contributed mainly to bring the sufferers thither'. (*Sheffield Iris*)

JULY 29TH

1885: One hundred and twenty paupers from the Wortley workhouse had a treat in place of their annual visit to the Ecclesfield Feast – they were given a pleasurable day's outing to the Wharncliffe Crags. The weather was bright and warm, and, although rain had been forecast, it managed to stay dry for most of the day. The party was conveyed in wagons, which arrived at the Crags at 1 p.m., when they all sat down to a very satisfying dinner. There was dancing on the green to a local band, which the elderly paupers enjoyed, and in which many of them joined in. A number of juvenile races then took place, until it was time for tea. There were tug of war teams as well as demonstrations of May Pole dancing. The successful competitors afterwards received their prizes, the gifts having been donated by Mr W. Dransfield of Penistone, the clerk to the Wortley Guardians of the Poor. On their return back to the workhouse, each inmate was given a little packet of tea, sugar or tobacco and the children were given sweets and nuts. The expenses of the day were covered by subscription and a large vote of thanks was given to the guardians. (*Sheffield Courant*)

JULY 30TH

1885: News reached the town today of the death of Revd John Harris (23) of Sheffield, who left the country more than a year ago to become a missionary in Central Africa. The news was received in a telegram from the mission in Zanzibar. A previous telegram baldly stating 'Harris died May 29th' had been received and his friends and relations waited anxiously for details of his death. It seems that Revd Harris had just reached Lake Tanganyika, where he was to begin his work, when he was struck down with fever and from which he died. Revd R. Wardlaw Thompson of the London Missionary Society, stated that the very popular Revd Harris 'was a young man with considerable promise who had been imbibed with true Christian zeal. The highest anticipation was held for the work he was to accomplish, and he was a man of great personal courage. He had a true "Livingstone" spirit and a manly disregarded of any difficulties of his position'. Revd Harris had been educated for the ministry at Rotherham College and had only been ordained at Garden Street Chapel in April of the previous year. He left a mother and two sisters. (*Sheffield Telegraph*)

JULY 31ST

1900: There appeared on this day a report of a 'Negro American' Bishop's visit to the Burngreave Congregational Church last evening. The Revd Alexander Walters of New York delivered an address on 'The trials and Achievements of the Coloured Race in America'. Mr Walters is a native of the southern states of America and is Bishop of the African Methodist Episcopal Church. Bishop Walters said that lynch law was prevalent to an alarming extent, and there was still a good deal to be done before all races could be equal. Bishop Walters delivered a lengthy address, in which the audiences were very much interested. 'The Negroes of America,' he said, 'could have nothing but words of praise and heartfelt thanks for the kind way the people of England had extended to them a helping hand in the abolition of slavery. He himself was once a captive and he well remembered when his mother, who had in some way displeased her master, was sold to another master for a sum of money.' He said that there were now 156 institutions for coloured people in the Southern states. A million dollars had been contributed towards the education of Negro's since their emancipation. (*Sheffield Weekly Telegraph*)

AUGUST 1ST

1842: A large crowd gathered on the New Circus to hear a lecture by Revd R.S. Bayley on the formation of a People's College. This establishment would be for the education of young people from the middle and working classes, of fourteen years of age and upwards. He said: 'The great mass of people were not educated, and this, as Members of Parliament had said, would bring the people to the borders of revolution. The government argued that setting up such schools would be expensive, but money could always be found for royal stables or the setting up of commissions of enquiry. But it was another thing when money was needed for the education of the people'. Revd Bayley proposed to open a college with eleven classes of students; one class to meet each morning and one to get together at night. The first would be for the rudimentary reading, writing and spelling classes. The others would include geography, mathematics, English and general history, English composition and public speaking, science, and natural history. A show of hands was called for and it was proved unanimously. Revd Bayley announced that he was ready to receive the names of interested students in Howard Street Chapel vestry. (*Sheffield Indpendent*)

August 2nd

1572: On this day, it seems that the Earl of Shrewsbury, by now growing tired of his prisoner Mary Queen of Scots, wrote to Her Majesty Queen Elizabeth I from Sheffield: 'Having these ten years been secluded from your most gracious sight and happy presence, which more grieveth me than any travail or discommodity that I have suffered in this charge that it hath pleased Your Majesty to put me in trust withal, I have taken the boldness most humbly to beseech Your Majesty that it may please the same to licence me for a fortnights' journey towards Your Majesties' most royal person to the end. You may by myself a true account of my said charge, and thereby know what my deservings are; wherein if I may (as I desire most earnestly) satisfy Your Majesty, it shall be unto me a great encouragement to continue the most faithful duty and careful service that I owe unto Your Majesty and shall yield to my life's end.' On the same day he wrote a letter to Secretary Walsingham, asking him to support his plea and telling him that during his absence he would leave Mr Wortley, one of the council at York, to take care of the Scottish Queen. (Bunker, B., *Portrait of Sheffield*, London, Hale Publishing, 1972)

AUGUST 3RD

1874: The Sheffield Court today heard of a 'heartless' man called Thomas Allen, who had been summoned by Miss Isabella Johnson for the maintenance of her illegitimate child. In the course of enquiries being made of Allen, it transpired that the defendant was a married man who already had a large family of young children. In extremely severe interrogation, the magistrate asked Miss Johnson if she had been aware that Allen was a married man, to which she replied that she 'certainly had not'. She told the magistrate that Allen had represented himself as a single man to her and her friends, and it was whilst he had been paying his addresses to her that he succeeded in seducing her and she had become pregnant. She had not seen him since the birth of the baby. On one occasion, she saw Allen on West Bar with some children, but he told her that they were his nieces and nephews, and that he was lodging with his sister for the time being. Allen did not turn up at court, but sent a letter admitting that the child was his and agreeing to pay Miss Johnson 2s a week in maintenance, which the bench agreed was a fair rate. (*Sheffield Register*)

AUGUST 4TH

1787: The Lord of Sheffield, the Duke of Norfolk and the townspeople had agreed in 1784 that an improved marketplace was desperately needed in the town. The rise in the numbers of townspeople during market days had proved the necessity of building one as soon as possible. Three years later, on the very same day, the local newspaper reported that the old market, which, 'used to be held in a confused irregular manner in the streets and which travellers have frequently complained of as dangerous and disagreeable, has now been replaced. The newly elegant marketplace, which is neatly graceful in appearance and commodious in its construction, contains the butchers, hucksters and part of the gardener's stalls and so on. Another part of the market holds the dealers in earthenware, metalwork and china products. Those selling fruit and vegetables stand in Paradise Square, a large convenient place in the centre of the town. By these agreeable regulations the streets have a better appearance and carriages pass free from interruption, without endangering the foot passengers.' The building itself was grandiose in its formation and was named the Fitzalan Market Hall. The Duke of Norfolk imposed a toll on the market traders before they could be permitted to sell their goods. (Leader, J.D., *The Records of the Burgery of Sheffield*, Sheffield Independent Press, 1897)

AUGUST 5TH

1829: An unnamed female servant living in Sheffield attempted to drown herself in the canal near the bridge at Attercliffe. The reason for the attempt was due to a dispute with a fellow servant, who claimed that she had lost a shilling. The woman was charged with taking the shilling, and it is this which is believed to have led to her brush with death. A witness named Osbourne observed her walking by the canal side, and he noted that she seemed very agitated. He therefore decided to watch her for a time. She did not attempt to jump into the canal whilst he was watching her, however, fortunately for her, he turned back to look in time to see her plunging into the water. He ran immediately to try to get her out of the water, but she had sunk to the bottom. He did not succeed in extricating her until a hay rake had been procured from a passer-by. She was afterwards taken to a house in Attercliffe, where she was very kindly treated, and was soon afterwards sufficiently recovered to be taken home in a carriage. (*Sheffield Independent*)

AUGUST 6TH

1795: A riot took place in Sheffield the previous evening. It seems that a party of military volunteers had argued with their colonel about arrears. Bystanders in Norfolk Street who did not like the volunteers – looking on them as instruments of oppression – joined in the argument and started to throw stones at them. Tempers rose and Colonel Althorpe, riding fast from Rotherham after dinner, drove his horse into the crowd in an attempt to disperse them. Accounts of his actions were conflicting. The *Courant,* a Tory paper, claimed that he merely rode about asking people to disperse. The *Iris*, however, said that he had 'plunged into the crowd with his horse among unarmed and defenceless people, wounding with his sword men, women and children promiscuously'. The Riot Act was read which had no effect on the crowd, and the volunteers were ordered to fire. Two people were killed and others wounded before the crowd finally dispersed. There were indications that the colonel was not entirely sober. A famous local singer, Joseph Mather, wrote and sang 'What the bloody tyrant meant/Was this murder without precedent'. (Walton, M., *Sheffield: Its Story and its Achievements*, Sheffield, Amethyst Press, 1984)

AUGUST 7TH

1872: A fire was discovered at the premises of Mr John James Eyre, a rope and tent cover manufacturer of Exchange Street, Sheffield. The fire had broken out in a store room over the shop, which had contained a large stock of items such as marquees, oil skin covers, cocoa mats and matting. The fire brigade was alerted and very quickly attended the scene. Mr Eyre arrived at about 8 p.m., when it seems that the fire was then under control. However, almost all the goods in the store room had been destroyed and the value of the stock was estimated to have a net value of £1,200. Thankfully, this was partially covered by insurance. (*Sheffield Times*)

AUGUST 8TH

1892: It was reported in the *Sheffield Independent* that 'George Smith will never earn a living as a thief unless he learns a few professional methods'. Smith was walking down South Street on Friday night, when he saw a number of hams hanging in the doorway of Edward Hill, a provisions merchant. Fancying some ham for his supper, he stole one. He was spotted by another George Smith, also a provision merchant of South Street. Smith, chased his namesake, who, encumbered by a 16lb ham, was easily run down and captured. The ham was returned by the guilty George Smith to Edward Hill. The prisoner was brought before the magistrates at the Town Hall on Saturday and charged with theft. He pleaded not guilty, blaming the theft on his being drunk. He was fined 20s, and, in default of paying the fine, was sent to prison for a month. (*Sheffield Independent*)

AUGUST 9TH

1931: It was announced at Sheffield on this day that a new product was in the process of being manufactured. Historically famed as the 'City of Steel', the city began to produce artificial gold. Successful experiments had been made on the casting of a non-ferrous alloy of aluminium and copper that had the appearance of gold. This alloy was being made to imitate the various carats of gold colour. The new metal was stainless and could be washed after use, standing up to very severe tests. It was expected that it would attain popularity as an alternative to gold, seeing as the manufacture was on established grounds. A successfully made full dinner set was even on show at the Cutler's Hall. The Master Cutler praised the new artificial gold metal, and told a reporter that he already had some interest from other firms about its manufacture. The metal could easily be moulded into plate, jewellery and other domestic items. It was said that the price of the metal worked out at about the same price as nickel silver, and thus was within the reach of all. (*The Times*)

AUGUST 10TH

1297: A Charter was granted to the people of Sheffield by Thomas de Furnival on this day. Thomas held the townspeople in high regard, calling them 'my free tenants of the town of Sheffield' and he gave their heirs 'all the tofts, lands and holdings which they hold of me' at the fixed annual rent of £3 8 9¼d. However, he reserved certain feudal dues, including the continued use of his manorial court, for his own disposal. The townsmen of Sheffield were also exempt from other feudal services, and were not required to pay tolls at the lord's market. It is clear from the wording of the charter that the people of the town were held in high esteem, so much so that they had already, for many years, held such privileges, which were then confirmed in writing. Sheffield never became a fully fledged medieval borough with its own mayor and corporation like that of Doncaster, instead being what historians call a 'seigniorial borough'. This entailed that the Lord of the Manor remained dominant, but the townspeople had some measure of independence. (Hey, D., *A History of Sheffield*, Carnegie Publishing Ltd, 1998)

August 11th

1857: It was reported that Mr William Wright of Holly Street, Sheffield, having successfully patented a self-acting water closet, had a very handsome specimen fitted up for the exhibition in the Museum of Patents at South Kensington, London. Externally, it appeared as a very handsome easy chair. On sitting down, a lever would be pressed, which admitted water silently into an air-tight vessel, the air of which was compressed by the entrance of the water. When the pressure was removed from the seat, as the user stood up, the compressed air forced the water from the vessel, flushing the basin completely. The machinery was ingenious yet simple, and was not liable to get out of repair. The exterior of the water closet was very stylish and adaptable, and could feasibly fit in 'workshops, simplistic cottages or the more ostentatious mansion'. *The Times* reported that this water closet 'would be very successful and likely to come into general usage in the foreseeable future.' (*The Times*)

AUGUST 12TH

1874: On this day, the Ecclesfield Paper Mill Company was summoned by Mr Robert Butterworth, the nuisance inspector, for the Wortley Union workhouse, for allowing foul water to run into a stream which ran along Ecclesfield Common. The matter was investigated by Mr Butterworth over several days, and he reported back to the workhouse guardians the following Monday. Evidence showed that the nuisance had existed since August of the previous year, and, despite the frequent complaints which had been made about it, nothing had been done to improve the matter. Mr Butterworth had taken samples, which showed that before the water reached the mill, the water was quite clean, but afterwards it contained thick, black sediment. The Sheffield Medical Officer of Health, Mr Drew, stated that the water was in a filthy state and subsequently was damaging to the health of the inhabitants of the town. It was important that the nuisance be abated because fever was at this time widespread in the village of Ecclesfield. The Bench made an order that the nuisance must be cleared with two weeks or the company would be fined. (*Sheffield Independent*)

AUGUST 13TH

1840: A report emerged in the newspapers about the abundance of fruit in the markets of Sheffield. It had been noted that the speed and cheapness of railway travel enabled the fruit growers of the South to send to the less productive counties of the North immense quantities of products from their orchards and hot houses. This system, which by this time had become fully established, was noted to be beneficial to both the producers and purchasers. To the former, it allowed a regular and steady demand, and, to the latter, it ensured a good supply in districts where fruit was not abundant. The reporter stated: 'Markets in Sheffield had an abundance of the finer varieties of fruit, including apricots, peaches and nectarines, which have been sent to this town from France via London. Thus, while the stone fruits were green in Sheffield gardens, residents could enjoy a ready supply from the warmer climates of the South'. (*Sheffield Iris*)

AUGUST 14TH

1914: At the height of suspicion at the beginning of the First World War, the conservative newspaper the *Sheffield Daily Telegraph* carried an editorial entitled 'The Germans Amongst Us'. The editorial called attention to the presence of a large number of German people in the United Kingdom. The paper reported that: 'Whilst it is undeniably a difficulty of the situation, given the present circumstances, it is becoming more of a problem that many of the Germans feel themselves the most acutely of all. A large number of them have dwelt for many years amongst us in perfect good faith and are quite harmless. Others it must be admitted are anything but, being held under suspicion by the Sheffield people, if the country goes to war. Many in the government are in favour of temporary internment, which is supported by the local and national newspapers. It is thought that if an invasion or even a raid should take place, it is a concern that thousands of Germans in this country might join the raiders, and swell their forces to very considerable proportion.' (*Sheffield Daily Telegraph*)

AUGUST 15TH

1876: A horrid discovery was made on this day at Sheffield Victoria Station, where it was reported that the body of a child had been found in the water closet connected with the third-class ladies' waiting room. It transpired that the child was male, and was found in a frightfully mutilated condition; cut into five pieces, the arms and legs having been severed at the joints and thighs. The child was thought to be nine or ten months old and had been killed about two days before his body was found. A young girl found the corpse, and told her mother, Mrs Louisa Barrow, that she had seen a strange parcel on the floor of a water closet. PC Walker, one of the station police, unwrapped the parcel and found the remains of the child, which were covered in a piece of skirt of a black and grey material. The body was taken to the Town Hall and the police began their investigations. Another girl, Mary Ann Brownhill, and a companion had also seen the parcel earlier and had rested their feet upon it, thinking that it was a hassock. (*Sheffield Independent*)

AUGUST 16TH

1839: It was announced in today's *Yorkshire Post* that the Sheffield Dragoons had been sent to Macclesfield to quell some disturbances there. Following an urgent dispatch from the commander of the force for the district at Nottingham to Captain Marten, which arrived late on Thursday night on the brilliant coach, the principle part of the Dragoons in their barracks found themselves marching at 2 a.m. on the morning of August 15th to Macclesfield. The Sheffield Yeomanry had therefore been called out to protect the town in the Dragoons absence. A large amount of them met on the evening of August 14th, and the remainder were to meet on the 15th. They were to be under the command of Captain Woodhead. It was expected that they would be quartered in the town, until the return of the Dragoons. The cause of their march to Macclesfield is reported to have been because riots had taken place there, which were not of a particularly serious nature. It was reported that upwards of twenty persons had been apprehended at Macclesfield and all had been remanded until they were brought before the magistrates. These were probably Chartist riots which, during the period of 1839 to 1840, affected most towns and manufacturing centres of the country. (*Yorkshire Post*)

AUGUST 17TH

1846: The local newspapers of this day reported that the Annual General Meeting of the Sheffield School of Art was to be held on the subsequent Wednesday evening, during which the newly appointed master, Mr Young Mitchell, would give an introductory address. Other annual meetings had previously been poorly attended, and it was often a great regret among those involved to see such little interest taken in the welfare of an institution of such vital importance to Sheffield. The *Sheffield Times* reported that: 'By their attendance at the meeting, the inhabitants generally, will have an opportunity of making themselves acquainted with the principles of this institution. The school has always had our warmest wishes for its success, feeling confident as we do, that it must ultimately raise the character of our manufacturers, by drawing closer together the bond which exists between them and art. We will only add that the annual subscription is so trifling, as to place it in the power of all who wish well to the arts and manufacturers of this country. We request that the numbers of the principal men of the town to add their names to the list. We look forward with confidence, and we trust that the annual report of next year will show our appeal has not been made in vain.' (*Sheffield Times*)

AUGUST 18TH

1829: On this day the beginning of the grouse shooting season was announced, which occasioned the usual influx of visitors to Sheffield. The *Sheffield Courant* reported: 'These gentlemen usually fixed their headquarters here and at the various inns in the vicinity of the moors around us. The birds are remarkably numerous and strong on the wing. We have heard of one gentleman who bagged on the first day twenty brace, and also a party of five who killed sixty brace. The coaches on Wednesday and yesterday were heavily laden with hampers of birds, for various members of the Royal Family and the Nobility. On the whole the sport has been good and has this year been enjoyed by a more than usual number of gentlemen. The Duke of Rutland is entertaining a party at Longshawe House, and B. Houndsfield Esq. has a party of friends in a tent on Bradfield Moors. We believe that on the Yorkshire Moors the broods are in great numbers. On the grounds of the Duke of Devonshire the number of birds in a brood are small, though in the best condition. It has been said that the grouse were never known either to be so numerous or so fine as during the present season.' (*Sheffield Courant*)

AUGUST 19TH

1843: On this day, a letter was printed regarding the bust of Sheffield poet James Montgomery, which had been commissioned by sculptor Edwin Smith for the Cutler's Hall. The letter from Mr Smith explained the circumstances in which the bust had been made. In order to get a good likeness, he had approached Mr Montgomery, who granted him a number of sittings. A number of gentlemen, on seeing the bust, agreed to promote a subscription for it to be made in marble, and the subscriptions would be limited to one guinea. When the bust was completed, it was taken to the National Exhibition at the Royal Academy in Trafalgar Square, London, where it remained until it was returned to Sheffield. Mr Smith then wrote the letter to the Cutler's Company in order to explain the delay of the bust. He stated: 'Allow me to present this tribute of respect of our revered and highly gifted townsman to the ancient corporation of which you are the head. I understand it is to be placed in that beautiful hall where meetings for social, benevolent and religious objects have so often been aided and delighted by this most Christian poet.' The bust can today be seen exhibited in the Cutler's Hall. (*Sheffield Independent*)

AUGUST 20TH

1859: A report in the *Sheffield Times* today detailed a woman's vicious attempt at taking her husband's life. The victim was a collier named Sullivan, living in the Old Ropery Park. The man's wife, Mary, had arranged to go with some friends to a village feast several miles away, and Sullivan had expressed his determination to accompany her. It appeared that she may have had reasons for preferring to go without her spouse, and told him that she had lent some of his Sunday garments to a friend. It was then that a violent altercation ensued, during which Mary picked up a knife and inflicted a severe wound to her husband's arm. Afterwards, she aimed a blow at his neck with the knife, but fortunately did not succeed in inflicting a serious injury. The poor fellow grappled with his wife to prevent her from stabbing him any more. A crowd was attracted by the noise of the fight, and one of the men came to Mr Sullivan's assistance and removed the knife from Mary. A constable was called, but the man refused to give his wife into custody. Medical aid was obtained and Sullivan then spent some time recovering. (*Sheffield Times*)

AUGUST 21ST

1876: A letter was published in the *Sheffield Independent*, in which the writer complains about the use of bad language by Sheffield locals:

> Sheffield, Aug 21. 1876
>
> Sir,
> There is one disgusting practice which is daily on the increase and little or no effort appears to be made by the authorities to put a stop to it. I refer to the abominable manner to which young couples (one of each sex) are continually insulted and annoyed by gangs of unprincipled fellows who frequent the streets and outskirts of Sheffield. A young lady and gentleman are now positively unable to go anywhere in the town without being compelled to listen to the most obscene and disgusting remarks from these ruffians. Should the insulters be remonstrated with, they either commence an assault on their remonstrators or subject them to still more abominable language. It really is time that something was done to put an end to this class of annoyance, as it seems most atrocious that ladies, and in fact mere girls, are compelled to hear such disgusting language. I think if our police authorities would put on a few more policemen in plain clothes we should soon experience a better state of things.
>
> A SUFFERER

(*Sheffield Independent*)

August 22nd

1795: 'A meeting of the Cutler's Company was interrupted today by a number of women with ribbons and cockades in their hats. They entered the room at the Cutler's Hall in which the gentlemen of the Corn Committee had assembled. They thanked the gentlemen most heartily for the great reduction which the committee had on that day made in the price of corn. The women then marched up in a body to the head of the table, and, addressing Dr Browne, the chairman of the committee, told him that they had brought a chaise to the door of the Cutler's Hall. They begged his leave to draw him through the principal streets of the town, to indicate the gratitude of the people of Sheffield. The doctor declined with honour, giving his reasons that "it would invert the order of things, and therefore it would be ungallant of him to accept". The women, having repeatedly and urgently preferred their petition to him and the other members of the committee, then retired, invoking blessings on those who had been the cause of the great and sudden reduction in the price of corn today.' (*The Sheffield Courant*)

AUGUST 23RD

1847: Local newspapers stated today that since taking on the chairmanship of the Manchester, Sheffield and Lincolnshire Railway, the Earl of Yarborough has shown great assiduity in all matters relating to railways. 'Within the last few weeks, his Lordship has traversed, in company with Mr Fowler (the eminent engineer of the company), the whole of the line of the works eastward of Sheffield. On Monday, his Lordship visited the Parkgate and Chapeltown works of Messrs Schofield and Co., in order to witness the manufacture of rails, the smelting of the ironstone, the casting of pig, the process of the paddling furnace, from which the iron comes out to be hammered into puddle bars and afterwards rolled into rails. In his speech at the meeting on Wednesday, his Lordship stated that when the whole system of railways, forming the Manchester, Sheffield and Lincolnshire Railway shall be complete, the cost including stations and stock will only be £17,000 per mile. He also alluded to the opinion of Mr George Stephenson; that a railway to be used as a turnpike road through agricultural districts would pay an ample profit on an expenditure of £12,000 a mile. His Lordship was thanked for his great attention to detail as chairman.' (*Sheffield Iris*)

AUGUST 24TH

1854: A report was published today detailing the misfortune of several townspeople who had been subject to a scam. A man who called himself Mr Barr rented a shop to use as an office, which he told the landlord was to teach photography. He said he had another shop, but couldn't use it for the time being and this was to be set up as a temporary office. In this makeshift office, he announced himself as a loan company of which 'H. Barr was the manager'. Notices were put up announcing that loans would be granted from £2.50 to £50, and larger loans on 'special agreement'. People applying for loans were asked for a few shillings, whilst enquiries were made into their character. It was thought that over two dozen people had been duped in this fashion. But the worst swindle was that of men applying to become clerks to the loan company, who were offered a considerable salary when they got the job. Needless to say they all got the job, and had to put down a sum of money – between £10 to £70 each – as security for their honesty. They were given a starting day on a Wednesday, and turned up to find Mr Barr had absconded with all the money. (*Sheffield Times*)

AUGUST 25TH

1937: Today it was announced that the 9,000-ton cruiser HMS *Sheffield* underwent its final trials in the North Sea, which proved successful. The *Sheffield* was built by Vickers Armstrong on Tyneside at the Walker Naval Yard and was shortly followed by her sister ship, the *Newcastle*. Both these ships were the first of this class of vessel to be completed at the shipyard and they cost £1.8 million. The *Sheffield* was launched by the Duchess of Kent on July 23rd 1936. The *Yorkshire Post* reported that: 'It was planned that, in October of 1937, HMS *Sheffield* will anchor off the docks at Immingham in order to receive gifts of plate and cutlery from the city of Sheffield. There is tremendous interest in the first warship to be named after the town. The women of Sheffield collected over £100 to buy a silk, Union Jack and a silk, white Ensign for the ship. A stainless steel ship's bell was also made at Sheffield's Hadfield works, which included the coat of arms of the city and was presented to the ship's crew. The cruiser, which has a cruising speed of 34 knots, will carry 12 x 6in and 8 x 4in guns as well as several smaller guns and six torpedoes.' (*Yorkshire Post*)

AUGUST 26TH

1844: Details of a day out in York for 400 students and subscribers from the People College were published today. The aim was that instruction could be combined with recreation at places of historical interest. From their rooms in Orchard Street, where the students were undertaking very intense courses of study, they set off for the station. It was there that they boarded a special train and filled ten carriages; the huge group arriving in York at noon. The weather was extremely kind to them during their day spent in York, allowing them to visit most of the historical sights. They broke into several groups and went to the many attractions, such as the castle, the Cathedral, Clifford's Tower and to walk along the city walls. After having refreshments at the Station Hotel, the group left on another special train from York, a few minutes before 7 p.m. and reached Sheffield at about 9.30 p.m. Many of the students expressed their gratitude to the organisers of the visit, and it was hoped that the group could visit York on another occasion. It was deemed that these outings would not only allow students to visit places of interest, but that they would also stimulate the students of the People College. (*Sheffield Independent*)

AUGUST 27TH

1845: The inhabitants of George Street were witness on this day to the testing of the Sheffield Fire Office's new and revolutionary fire escape. The apparatus consisted of a ladder that could be adjusted to a number of convenient lengths. The head of the ladder was furnished with wheels and a pulley through it which runs a strong rope. One end of this was furnished with a strap, and the other was held by the men at the foot of the apparatus. When the pulley was raised to a window on the third storey of a building, several of the firemen, who were in the building, were easily lowered to the ground by means of this strap, and were secured around their waist by the men holding the rope at the foot of the ladder. The mode of this escape had one advantage over that used at Manchester and Liverpool some time in 1845, where the parties escaped a burning building by sliding down a length of sacking, which had been attached to the window, and the other end held by persons in the street. It was agreed that this sacking would be liable to be set on fire, whereas using the ladder and rope in this fashion would avoid this danger. (*Sheffield Independent*)

AUGUST 28TH

1756: A letter was sent to the editor of the *Sheffield Iris* on this day, in which the recent Sheffield riots were discussed: 'I suppose you have heard what terrible confusion this town has been in for days past, the mob carrying all before them and breathing nothing but fury and destruction, On Thursday night, they attacked Pond Mill, pulling all the slates off, although they did little damage beyond that whilst only taking two loads of corn. Yesterday the Marquis of Rockingham and Justice Battie was in the town and they constituted ten new constables. A company of stout, able men assembled last night well armed with bludgeons, guns and bayonets and knocked down all before them that they knew to be part of the gang. They patrolled the town and seized the ringleaders, some were in bed and some were in the streets. They brought them as prisoners to the Town Hall this morning before the justices. All the best of the people in the town is ready for its defence and the mob are not able to stand them all and consequently the town is, at present, very quiet.' (Leader, R.E., *Sheffield in the Eighteenth Century,* Sheffield, Sir W.C. Leng & Co., 1905)

AUGUST 29TH

1680: Sir John Reresby recalled on this day his attendance to the Cutler's feast at the invitation of the Master Cutler, Jonathon Webster, along with his wife and family and some of his close neighbours: 'I took with me the number of nearly thirty horses. The Master and Wardens attended by an infinite crowd met me at the entrance to the town, with music. I alighted from my coach and went afoot with the Master to the hall where we had an extraordinary dinner; but it was all at the charge of the Corporation of Cutlers. In the afternoon, the burgesses of the town invited me and all my company to a treat of wine at the tavern, where we were well entertained.' The feast was one of the earliest ever held, although it is known from the records that in 1649 the Master, Robert Brelsforth, was allowed the sum of £1 10s towards the cost of five dinners. It was the custom for these feasts to contain superb food and entertainment and for the Master to personally go and invite guests to the feast. (Vickers, J.E., *Old Sheffield Town: An Historical Miscellany*, Sheffield, Hallamshire Press, 1999)

August 30th

1844: The *Sheffield Independent* stated today that, 'for the past few days, the inhabitants of the town have been favoured with a high treat from the able lectures of Mr Spencer at the Sheffield Theatre, on the subject of mesmerism. Over such a short time, hundreds of local people have visited the theatre and been entertained by this revolutionary new science.' The lectures held not only a curious fascination, but Mr Spencer demonstrated interesting experiments on a number of patients to illustrate the subject. 'The demonstrations possessed a very great interest and were so satisfactory as to convince many of the truth of a science, regarding which, they had hitherto remained sceptical. Mr Spencer was unquestionably a gentleman of decided talent and literary acquirements, and was a great enthusiast on the subject of mesmerism. He devoted much time to studying and therefore understanding it very well. It was indeed a subject which appeared well worthy of investigation, and it must be rapidly forcing itself upon the attention of all reflecting minds. It is understood that Mr Spencer will proceed with his lectures for just two more days, before continuing to his engagements in Nottingham.' (*Sheffield Independent*)

AUGUST 31ST

1872: An incident which caused a soldier to be sent to prison for a three-month sentence for what was no more than a prank was printed today. A private in the 5th Dragoon Guards was billeted in the Crescent Inn, Sheffield, and whilst 'in his cups' wanted to make himself 'free' with the young lady of the establishment. He tried to kiss her, and then kissed her mother when she tried to intervene. For this misdemeanour, he was charged with 'assault' by the Bench, who sentenced him to three months in the Wakefield House of Correction without the option of a fine. This sentence was felt to be so unfair that, when passing through the town, the officers and soldiers of his regiment band were forbidden to play by their officer in command. In such a case like this, a small fine of two or three guineas was usually considered for such a trivial crime. (*Sheffield Times*)

SEPTEMBER 1ST

1854: 'The erection of the monument to local poet Ebenezer Elliott, opposite the Post Office, was completed today. Elliott was known as the 'Corn Law Rhymer' and although he was born in Rotherham, he later moved to Sheffield where he spent the rest of his life. The sculpture was visited throughout the week whilst it was being erected, and, on the day of its unveil, there was a large concourse full of spectators to see its magnificence. It is, however, generally admitted that the statue is not a striking likeness to the poet, and considering the lack of reward and resources offered to its creator, Mr Neville Burnard, this is only what might have been expected. He had never seen Elliott, and the portraits that were supplied to him were said to have been very vague and varying likenesses. There are some, however, who knew Elliott well and pronounced the likeness of the statue to be quite accurate. As a work of art, we are sure Mr Burnard had no cause to fear criticism. The statue, which was cast in bronze, sat on a pedestal of granite from the Rivelin Valley, which Elliott loved so much.' The statue was removed from its place in the High Street in 1874 to its existing position in Western Park. (*Sheffield Free Press*)

September 2nd

1828: 'Today Mr Green, the aeronaut, made his 61st aerial voyage from Hyde Park cricket ground to where enormous crowds were attracted. Early in the morning, the balloon was charged with 20,000ft of gas, in the yard adjoining the Sheffield Gas Works, and it was afterwards conveyed to the cricket ground in a cart. There were many young children following the cart as it went on its journey. Mr Green spent some of the journey making a number of partial attempts at a flight, for the gratification of a few ladies and gentlemen, at a cost of 1s each. At half past ten, the streets and the surrounding hills were crowded with anxious spectators, and the air was brimming with anticipation. At about 3.30 p.m., Mr Green stepped up to the balloon, and, after the necessary arrangements had been made, the cords were cut and the balloon rose majestically into the air, taking a southerly direction. It was only perceptible to the eye for about three minutes, after which it passed into a thick cloud. When it had risen about 100 yards, Mr Green dropped a parachute to which was suspended a small basket containing a cat, which fell near the New Hospital Chapel. Mr Green affected his descent at about 8 p.m. in a field near Beauchief Abbey.' (*Sheffield Iris*)

September 3rd

1830: On this day, a young man named Davy was arrested for stealing on a massive scale from his employers, Messrs Rodgers & Sons. He had been employed in the packing department and had concealed items on his person, from orders he was making up. When the items were reported missing, he assured his employers that he had in fact packed everything and it must be a mistake. He also had to take parcels to the post office for delivery, and he sometimes packed them with goods, and took them home. His rooms were searched after his arrest and almost a wagon full of items was found, which were later identified by his employers as being stolen. Parcels of goods were found with sham addresses written on them. He was engaged to be married, and the house of his fiancé was examined and stolen items were also found there, although the family was cleared of any guilt. Such was the arrogance of this young thief that he had spent a lot of money on fashionable clothes, which his employers later realised they were paying for. He was due to be examined on this day, and it was hoped the example would not be lost upon young men holding similar positions as he lately occupied. (*Sheffield Courant*)

SEPTEMBER 4TH

1899: For the first time today, electric trains ran in Sheffield. *The Times* reported that 'the city of Sheffield has discarded horse traction in favour of the overhead electric system.' The first of the sections, from the residential section of Nether Edge through the centre of the city and on to Attercliffe and Tinsley, were formally opened by the Lord Mayor. The Mayor was roundly criticised for starting the new system by taking the members of the corporation and its representatives for a round of test rides at a charge of 4*d*. All agreed that there should be some kind of public inauguration of a system, which, it was deemed, would be of incalculable benefit to the city. The starting of the electric tram was an immense sensation; hundreds of people thronged the routes which the trams were due to take. The tram system was judged to be both clean and cheap. Almost everyone could afford to use the trams when the price of a reasonable distance was only a halfpenny. The crowded city centre could now transport people to healthy suburbs. Thanks to the 'impractical radicals' of a dozen years before, modern projects which were beneficial to the city were beginning to come true. (*The Times*)

SEPTEMBER 5TH

1848: 'Children and teachers from the Park and Norfolk Street Sunday Schools were given permission to pay a visit to the Sheffield Botanical Gardens. The visit had been arranged between the Education Committee and the committee of the Botanical Gardens. It is supposed that there were almost 800 children in the group not including the teachers, and they arrived in carts at the gardens just after noon. The day was beautiful and fine and the children, judging from the joyous aspects of every countenance, appeared as delighted and happy as they well could be. It was really a treat to them, and will long be remembered with pleasure by many, when they are no longer children. Going through the gardens, the teachers were asked the names of many of the flowers and plants by the children. By the admirable arrangements of the curator, they were permitted to pass through the conservatories, which we are happy to say they did without causing any damage to the plants or the flowers. After walking around the garden, they assembled on the hill, where they had some refreshments before being allowed an hour's play time. The group returned home at about 5 p.m., and all were greatly delighted with their afternoon's excursion.' *(Sheffield Independent)*

SEPTEMBER 6TH

1828: 'On the evening of this day, a meeting was held regarding the establishment of a self-supporting dispensary for the town. The Master Cutler had previously written to His Grace the Duke of Norfolk, Rt Hon Earl Fitzwilliam and the Rt Hon Lord Wharncliffe requesting that they become patrons of the institute. Both of the latter agreed to accept to become patrons with the greatest pleasure, and Lord Wharncliffe stated his intention to become a subscriber. From the Duke of Norfolk, no answer had been received, but the readiness on his part to sanction and support the institute was confidently anticipated. All were sure that his Grace would not disregard any appeal made to him on behalf of his poor and afflicted townsmen. Having three such distinguished patrons, the committee hoped that the self-supporting dispensary would obtain the support to which it was entitled, and become a real blessing to the poor of this town. In order to start off the subscriptions, the Master Cutler announced that a collection had been made at St Bolderstone's chapel and a total of £2 11 6½d had been received. It was hoped that a subscription list would soon be started, which would be supported by some of the principle gentlemen of the town.' (*Sheffield Mercury*)

SEPTEMBER 7TH

1839: 'Today, at a meeting of the Brewster Sessions for Sheffield, applicants from the town who had collected together in order to renew their licenses, were warned by Mr Wrightson that, according to a clause in the Act of Parliament of 57th Geo. III, which, although not generally known, was still in full force. He took this opportunity to warn them as there were assembled a great number of publicans and magistrates. This clause referred to persons holding licensed houses, allowing illegal meetings and clubs assembling within their precincts. The Act gave the magistrates the power to revoke licenses on proof of being given of the holding of such meetings, which as landlords they would be seen as encouraging them. The magistrates thought it their duty to remind landlords in consequence of late proceedings in different parts of the country. Any person convicted of allowing illegal meetings connected with the Chartists, or any other illegal nature, the license would be forfeit. He thought it necessary to point out their attention in this matter, in order that they might be on their guard, for the Law would certainly be allowed to take its full course and in all cases the licenses of the parties would be suspended.' (Leader, R.E., *Sheffield in the Eighteenth Century*, Sheffield, Sir W.C. Leng & Co., 1905)

SEPTEMBER 8TH

1848: 'It was announced today that a series of lectures would be given by P.F. Aiken Esq. of Bristol on the French Revolution, in the Council Hall for the members of the Athenaeum. Mr Aiken stated in the first lecture that he would discuss the impact of the Kings of France on the revolution. He said the extreme corruption which existed in France before the revolution portended great convulsions. Added to this was the personal profligacy of the courts of France for several generations, which had debased the whole kingdom. Parliaments had little power and the monarch was exalted to absolutism. Before his death, the great absolutist monarch, King Louis XIV, told his son on his deathbed that he was 'too fond of war and lavish expenditure'. He urged his son to give relief to his people. But the reign of Louis XV had the evils of his father's reign, albeit without any of its brilliancy and power. Our nation should have been counted as happy to whom the sovereign on the throne was a safeguard of freedom. Our own sovereign had so merited respectful attachment from her people that she was valued and admired throughout the land. The hall reverberated to cries of "God save the Queen".' (*Sheffield Iris*)

September 9th

1809: On this day, an account was written which complimented the way in which the Cutler's Feast was carried out. The Cutler's Company was set up as a charitable enterprise for the poor of the district, but, once a year, a veritable feast was held for the company themselves. The account stated that: 'the master, wardens, searchers and assistants of the Cutler's Company took their usual oaths on entering their respective officers for the ensuing year. In complement to Richard Brightmore Esq., the Master Cutler, about one hundred and seventy gentlemen dined with the Company at their hall. Many excellent songs were sung and the day concluded in the utmost harmony. Mr Barton of the Barrack Tavern furnished the dinner and wines and conducted the entertainment with great propriety. In the evening there was an assembly at the Rooms on Norfolk Street.' It was also reported that the event took place in the afternoon, so that 'those of our forefathers who could walk steadily after the Master Cutler profuse hospitality; which in those days was considered the mark of a gentleman, could attend.' It is important to realise that at a time where impropriety was so frowned upon, a person's conduct was a matter of the utmost importance. (*Sheffield Courant*)

SEPTEMBER 10TH

1831: Accounts of the Coronation celebrations of King William IV and Queen Adelaide, which had been held in Sheffield, were published today. 'Demonstrations of loyalty and affection were seen, and health of the new King and Queen were toasted to. The Master Cutler, the magistrates and men of public bodies went to the New Market attended by banners and bands of music. Precisely at twelve o'clock, a detachment of the Royal Horse Artillery was joined by a squadron of 13th Hussars, who led the parade out of the marketplace and across Blonk Bridge. Despite a heavy fall of rain, the crowds were not deterred while 100 gentlemen were served dinner at the Corn Market. Master Cutler, Thomas Asline Ward, proposed the health of His Majesty, and told his dinner companions that he remembered both George III and George IV, and that he hoped that William IV would command the affections of the people of Sheffield. He said that George III was not a peaceful monarch, George IV could not be thought of as a personable man, but at least he brought a peaceful reign. The new King was superior to his predecessors and also a patriot and a reformer.' (*Sheffield Iris*)

SEPTEMBER 11TH

1851: It was reported today that a cannon exploded suddenly with great violence during a test fire. The makers of cannons in the Sheffield area were obliged to test them before delivering them to the buyers. Some workmen employed at Messrs Ellen's Wheel on Sylvester Street, Sheffield, were firing a cannon in this fashion when, with a loud explosion, it shattered. Large pieces of iron were flung around the yard and one large piece, weighing several pounds was hurled 100 yards away; it was later found in the yard of Mr Sykes' manufactory next door, which was fortunately empty at the time. Incredibly, no workmen were killed or injured during the explosion. Mr Sykes laid the matter before the magistrates, and produced a portion of the cannon which had landed on his premises. He told the magistrates, 'That piece alone could have felled a number of men, if there had been any in the area.' He further stated that he knew that some boys were firing some pieces of cannon that day in Doctor's Field, and suggested that a number of police be sent to the area, in case a similar accident should occur again. (*Sheffield Times*)

September 12th

1848: 'Great disquiet was expressed today at the shareholder's meeting of the Manchester, Sheffield and Lincolnshire Railway. The closure of the Sheffield was proposed, and a move to Manchester was suggested. The report had been circulating for some time and the shareholders stated that it would be of the greatest inconvenience, not only for business, but also to the people of the town itself. So strongly has this subject been felt in Sheffield, that a memorial to the directors has been very respectfully signed during the last few days. It was presented yesterday by the Mayor, Wilson Overend Esq. and Alderman Dunn. The memorial had been signed by merchants, bankers, tradesmen, share brokers and other inhabitants pointing out that the station at Sheffield was in the direct centre of the line. It also mentioned that being contiguous to the junction with the Midland railway; it was well placed for rapid communication, an essential factor in business. Begging the directors to consider the wishes of its shareholders, the memorial asked for their views to be taken into consideration. When it was submitted there had been a full board of directors with the Earl of Yarbrough in the chair.' (*Sheffield Mercury*)

September 13th

1838: An inquest was held today into a serious incident at the Surrey Music Hall the previous night, during which five people were crushed to death. 'The verdict of the coroner's jury was that Ellen Staley and three others were suffocated during their attempt to escape from the Surrey Music Hall following a cry of "fire" from an audience member. But whether such a cry was raised in consequence of the firing of a pistol, or an explosion of gas or from what other cause, no satisfactory evidence has been adduced to the jury. Alfred Dale, another victim, was killed by jumping from a window during the same panic. There was a strong conflict of opinion on what happened; certainly, there was a flash of light and a report, although there was no trace of a gas explosion. The incident didn't detract the visitors as it was reported that the Music Hall was re-opened again tonight and was filled in every part. Before the performance, the manager, Mr Youdan, offered his regret and sympathy to the families of the deceased that such an incident had taken place. He asked that, if such an incident should occur again, that people remain in their seats until the matter could be thoroughly investigated.' (*Sheffield Independent*)

September 14th

1885: An announcement was made in the *Daily Telegraph* that a local girl had gone missing from Sheffield. 'The report was filed yesterday to the Sheffield police that Miss Bessie Johnson of Jenkin Road, had been missing since Monday September 7th. The missing girl (16) was a student teacher at the National Day School on Hoyle Street, and was preparing for an examination which was to take place in October. The girl was reported missing by her sister, Miss Mary Johnson of Leeds. Bessie had been sent to stay with her sister for a rest, after complaining to her parents that she had too much studying to do. She was described as being stout in build and 4ft 10in tall. Her hair was light brown and cut short with a parting on her right side, and her complexion fair. When she left home, she was dressed in a dark brown cashmere shawl, trimmed with black velvet and a brown ulster with a small cape attached, a black chip hat trimmed with black velvet and white poppies, and high topped leather boots. The Sheffield and Leeds police requested that anyone with any knowledge of Miss Johnson must come forward.' (*Daily Telegraph*)

September 15th

1861: A letter was published in the *Sheffield Independent* regarding the nuisance of the unfeasibly large number of dogs in Sheffield. The letter stated:

To the Editor,

During my recent visit to London, I was struck with the remarkable favourable contrast between that city and Sheffield. Here, the intolerable number of dogs, most of them existing for no earthly good, is notorious. In London, in the course of a week, I saw but *two*: one was affectionately nursed in the arms of a lady, and the other, a ferocious looking animal, in the charge of a man equally forbidding. I saw none that were permitted to run at large to the danger and annoyance of foot passengers, as is the case hourly in our town. Amongst the many abuses that call for removal surely the dog nuisance is the most monstrous. It struck me that if London could be spared the plague of useless dogs, why not Sheffield? The notice issued by our worthy Mayor had but little effect, and however ungracious the duty, I hope that the parties in authority will not fail to deal with the subject as the case requires. I would recommend an application to the city authorities, as there is no doubt that their remedy for the nuisance is truly a most effective one,

Yours truly, ANTI-CANIS

(*Sheffield Independent*)

September 16th

1851: Reports of the spontaneous combustion of a hayrick were published in local Sheffield newspapers on this day. It seems that the hayrick belonging to Mr Slagg, farmer of Sheffield Park, had caught fire on Sunday night. Information was passed to the police and the fire brigade, who hastened to the spot to render any assistance. On their arrival, they found that there was a great danger of the stack setting others alight. They therefore covered the rest with tarpaulin and wet blankets, with the exception of a very small stack close to the fire, which they removed altogether. The only water available was from a pool which lay 300 yards off, so a delay was experienced in tackling the fire. After spraying the water onto the stack, several hours passed before the blaze was brought under control. Due to the fear that it might burst into flames again, the stack was totally dismantled and taken away. An investigation was made by late afternoon, when it was thought that the fire had started by the hay being too green when it was stacked. The fire could be seen for miles around, and at one time it was estimated that there were over 2,000 people spectating and helping the firemen to control the fire. (*Sheffield Free Press*)

September 17th

1885: A case of utter depravity was unfolded in Sheffield today when two little girls with the surname Johnson were found wandering in the area of Gibraltar Street yesterday by PC Bailey. They told the constable that they had been thrown out of the house by their mother, and he took them to the Town Hall. The mother, Kate, was sent for and she stood next to the two children and it was clear that she was intoxicated. A workhouse relieving officer told them that the mother had discharged herself from the workhouse on Thursday, and the sum of 5s was given to her. The same night, a constable took the children back to the workhouse, as they had been found on the streets. On Saturday the mother appeared and took them out of the workhouse once more. It seems that she went to the house of a man she knew and he took her in, but turned the children out. The Mayor came to the decision that, 'we must give up the children to the mother, but I must caution her that she must lead a different life. If the children have to go into the workhouse, she should go with them.' The life she was leading was deemed to be most disgraceful. (*Sheffield Post*)

SEPTEMBER 18TH

1830: The state of trade in Sheffield was discussed on this day. The *Sheffield Iris* stated that: 'Amidst revolution and rumours of revolutions abroad and the reports of ministerial changes at home, it is gratifying to notice in the papers generally, a diminution of complaints of the state of trade, In some instances, a direct assurance that the satisfactory improvements in the local business of certain towns and districts, is taking place. We are highly gratified and happy to believe from that from observation and report, that this is the case with trade and manufacture in Sheffield. The workmen in the different branches of our staple trade may be said to be generally employed at wages, which if they do not in every case enable large families to obtain all the comforts, leave them in the majority of instances in no want of the necessaries of life. There seems rather to be a steady, well bottomed, progression from one stage of amendment to another; and although the steps are hardly perceptible in detail, while the aggregate movement seems favourable, we are, on the whole, better satisfied than if the changes were more sudden, lest in that case it might lead to some injudicious speculation and as a consequence injurious reaction.' (*Sheffield Iris*)

SEPTEMBER 19TH

1803: 'Tonight was held a meeting of the Burgery of Sheffield at the Tontine Inn. Subscriptions were opened by the inhabitants of the town for the purpose of the raising of a Volunteer Corps for Sheffield. The previous Volunteer Corps had been disbanded on May 21st 1802. Now the Burgesses feel that the establishment of such a Corps will be of most important service in this perilous crisis [the Napoleonic War]. It was also resolved that thanks be given to Lt Col Fenton for his assiduous attention to the discipline of the Sheffield Volunteer Corps during the last war, and it is hoped that he will once more take command of the new Corps. It was therefore resolved that two of this body of Trustees be commissioned to procure a charger, and to present it fully caparisoned to Lt. Col Fenton, as a token of civic thanks. It was also resolved they will use their best endeavours to procure a proper parade ground, as near to the town as maybe, for regular exercise of such Corps.' On August 1st it was later resolved that the charger presented to Lt. Col. Fenton proved 'unsteady and unfit for the purpose' and that a more suitable charger be procured. (Leader, J.D., *The Records of the Burgery of Sheffield*, Sheffield Independent Press, 1897)

September 20th

1854: Today it was announced that a public meeting was to be held in Sheffield for the purpose of considering sending an address to Her Majesty. A reporter noted that: 'It was hoped that the memorial would express the lack of confidence that the people of Sheffield had in the administration of that time, in the face of the Crimean War. It was suggested that the meeting would be called for a week on the following Monday. It was hoped that when the Mayor, Alderman Carr, convened the meeting, that the people of the town would give their support to sign the memorial as numerously as possible, headed by the Mayor. It was expected that he would preside, should he have recovered from the effects of a then-recent severe accident, which occurred when he was driving his brougham through the town. Many hoped that this would be the case, and the people of Sheffield could be given an opportunity to raise their objections to Her Majesty. The people hoped that by the time the address would be submitted to Her Majesty, the wording would already be agreed upon. There was little doubt that the address conveyed the unmistakable patriotism for which Sheffield was renowned for.' (*Sheffield Free Press*)

September 21st

1861: A description of Sheffield as it appeared in *The Builder* was published on this day under the series entitled 'The Conditions of Our Chief Towns'. These articles deliberately sought out the worst aspects of the borough and portrayed them in an unforgiving light; yet they took no notice of the burgeoning industry or the sudden rise in population of Sheffield. Regarding Sheffield it stated that: 'The narrow streets rise and fall in the most irregular manner... a thick, pulverizing haze is spread out over the city which the sun, even in the dog days, is unable to penetrate, save by a lurid glaze which had the effect of imparting to the green hills and golden corn fields in the high distance, the ghostly appearance of being whitened as with snow... The three rivers sluggishly flowing through the town, have made the conduits of all imaginable filth and at one particular spot... positively run blood. These rivers are polluted with dirt, dust, dung and carrion, the embankments are ragged and ruined: here and there overhung with privies: and often the site of ash and offal heaps – most desolate and sickening objects.' The article concluded that Sheffield was a town where all authority was so divided 'that there is virtually no authority at all.' (Hey, D., *A History of Sheffield*, Carnegie Publishing, 1998)

September 22nd

1890: A report about the accidental shooting of a father by his son was heard in the town today. The deceased, Mr W.B. Hamer, who had been employed for nineteen years by Messrs Wm Cooke and Co., went with his son to his mother's farm at Deepdale near Newport, Salop for a short weekend break. The following day after breakfast, the pair had gone out together, and the son (19) was carrying a loaded gun. They had not gone far when a shot rang out and the son found his father had been shot in the groin and, two hours, later he died. Late that evening, Mr H.J. Appleyard received the following telegram from his son: 'Horrified to say Pa met with a fatal gun accident. Break awful news gently at home'. The following morning, Mr Appleyard communicated the painful news to Mrs Hamer, and they both proceeded to Deepdale. On the Saturday afternoon, an inquest was held and a verdict of death by misadventure was decided. The news of Mr Hamer's untimely death created a great shock in Sheffield, especially amongst his numerous Wesleyan friends and at Messrs Cooke and Co. Mr Hamer (43) left behind a widow and eight children. (*Sheffield Star*)

September 23rd

1830: On this day was reported that an individual had died in a house on Sheffield Park: 'the person's history exhibits one of those singular aberrations of resolutions which occasionally characterize our race'. About three years ago, a smart-looking young fellow solicited and received employment from Mr Heywood, who then managed a farm in the Park, which was owned by the master of the poorhouse. He remained with this employer for two years and then went to live with Mr Ashmore, likewise in the Park. Among his other duties, he was to take charge of several horses. A short time before his death, he was taken ill and removed to the new workhouse. There, he was placed under the care of a surgeon, who was surprised to find that his patient was, in fact, female. Upon further enquiry, it was found that her name was Martha Royston. Several years ago, having suffered the disgrace of giving birth to an illegitimate child, she determined to abandon the garb of her sex and assume that of a man; and for a number of years she took her place with the scythe, the barrow or the team without fearing a competitor in the field or the road. She died of typhus fever aged thirty. (*Sheffield Iris*).

September 24th

1840: On this day, it was announced in the *Sheffield Mercury* on the subsequent Monday, the Sheffield, Manchester and Lincolnshire Railways were starting to run railway excursions to Leeds: 'We trust the weather will be favourable and the passengers so numerous as to induce the Company to repeat these trains periodically. As an experiment the fares are so reduced that even the poorest families will be able to enjoy a day out. These excursions will be a boon to people wishing to visit their friends in Leeds, who will take advantage of an opportunity to visit the shops and thereby bring revenue to Leeds. If this venture is a success, we are assured by the Railway Company that other excursions will follow and soon all the towns in the West Riding will be readily available to the people of Sheffield. It has long been understood that travelling by rail is the most comfortable and safest way to travel. It will be observed that the Company makes a distinction between the first and second class carriages. We have no doubt that this will be advantageous to the Company and add to the comfort of its passengers.' (*Sheffield Mercury*)

September 25th

1850: 'The second group of women from the Female Emigration Society boarded the *William Hyde* to proceed to Port Adelaide from Sheffield. It is speculated that there were only twenty-one women in this party, and it was stated that the group would be the last to go out this season. The Emigration Committee asked to receive some intelligence of the success of the first batch which went out on the *Culloden* several months ago before they send any more to that corner of the world. Upon their being taken onboard, the members of the party were taken to the cabin prepared for them. The wife of MP Mr Stuart Wortley called out each girl by name, and gave her a printed list of rules of conduct during the voyage. The rules reminded the girls that "it was only by cheerfulness and good temper and obedience to the regulations, that the comfort of the whole party could be maintained". The Rt Hon Sydney Herbert gave a few kind words to the emigrants, and he asked that they each write a letter to the committee on their welfare on arrival in their new country. He also gave them "Gods blessing which would afford them their future success in life".' (*Sheffield Independent*)

September 26th

1874: A newspaper article announced that the chief constable of Sheffield Police had over the last few days taken out summonses against many people for fortune telling, because of the large number of complaints he had received. He stated that 'offences under the Vagrant Act of George IV made it a felony for persons to pretend or to profess to tell fortunes. The first case was a married woman living in Charlotte Street, charged with having on August 11th pretended to tell fortunes'. The defence, Mr Patterson stated that 'the fortune telling business had been going on in the town for some years, and that a lot of weak-minded people had been taken in by such persons'. He pointed out, however, that there are two parties involved – the fortune teller and the client, who were composed of all classes, and all descriptions of people. He said: 'It was a great pity that there was no law against the people who had their fortunes told'. He said that his client was pleading guilty to the charge, but she had told him that the day after the summons was served, her yard was 'inundated' with people begging and entreating her to tell their fortune. The magistrate told her that he would bind her over with sureties for good behaviour. (*Sheffield Independent*)

SEPTEMBER 27TH

1877: Today, Sheffield welcomed the arrival of General Grant of America. The General spoke about the men from Sheffield who had gone to America, and helped to build up the manufacture of the country, inviting all the men of Sheffield to do likewise. However, it seems that the good General was not welcomed by all Sheffield people, and that there were a few conspicuous absences due to trade differences in the steel industry. It seems that the British had restrictions imposed on what they could import from America, which some manufacturers took exception to. General Grant stated that he 'had wanted to come and see what the older generations call "the old country", and, instead of an agricultural town, he had found a town completely modern with streets, churches, schools, houses as well as enormous trade halls, libraries and factories'. It was later reported that the following day, on September 28th, that he would visit the works of Messrs Joseph Rodgers & Sons, which was known the world over for its cutlery. Also, he was to visit the works of Messrs Cammell and Co. to see the old file and steel products as well as the more modern industry of armour plating. The Mayor thanked General Grant for his kind words, and 'trusted that he would enjoy his stay'. (*Sheffield Post*)

September 28th

1866: A very sad case was published today involving a local woman attempting to starve herself to death. Mrs Gower, had been deserted by her husband fifteen months before, and since that time had been employed in selling newspapers. For about a week prior to her death, she was not seen by her neighbours, but they could hear her moving around the house, so were not concerned initially. After a week had passed, they grew concerned and called in a constable, who, unable to gain admittance, went up a ladder to the first-floor bedroom. The woman was lying on the bed as if dead, but when he climbed in through the window, she demanded to know what he was doing there. She told him that she wished to be left alone and that 'she was ready to die'. She was removed to the workhouse and £37 10s in gold was found in her bed. She was weak and emaciated and somewhat wild in her face. It appears that the woman was obsessively clean and her landlord had gone into the house with wet shoes on, and since that time she refused to open her door to anyone, or to let anyone else into the house. It was doubtful whether she would recover. (*Sheffield Times*)

September 29th

1850: The Theatre Royal opened for the season on this evening under the management of Mr Charles Dillon. The gallery and pit were well filled, but the boxes were almost empty. After the band had played an overture, the curtains rose and displayed a new set drop representing the triumph of Britannia, which pleased the 'gods' so much that they sang 'Rule Britannia' in full chorus. Mr Dillon then appeared to speak an opening address, and was received with great and prolonged applause. Pieces from selected shows were acted for the occasion such as *The Musketeers*, *Richard III* with Mr Henry Cooke as Gloucester, and, of course, *Romeo and Juliet*. The appointment of the stage was made with greater care than usual, and, with the exhibition of several new scenes by Mr B. Tannett, there was evidence of a desire in the management to carry out much needed improvements in the theatre. The evening was spoiled, however, by the uproarious conduct of certain individuals in the gallery, and, 'we are persuaded that if efficient means be not taken to enforce order in all parts of the house, the interests of the Theatre will be materially injured.' (*Yorkshire Post*)

September 30th

1902: 'Lord Kitchener was today presented with the honorary Freedom of the City of Sheffield. In creating an officer of the Imperial Forces a freeman of the cutlery centre, the Corporation were not content to hand to Lord Kitchener the burgess certificate, but they also accompanied it with munificent gifts – including a case of cutlery and a silver dinner service, on which was inscribed his crest. In anticipation of his visit, the leading thoroughfares were decorated and there was a large display of bunting between the railway station and the Town Hall. Lord Kitchener arrived at about 12.30 p.m., and he was met at the station by a detachment of the Sheffield Volunteer Artillery, which formed a guard of honour. Sixty troopers of the Yorkshire Dragoons were also on duty to act as an escort. The train arrived and Lord Kitchener, in the uniform of a general, was welcomed by the Lord Mayor. The party travelled in coaches to the Town Hall, where despite the rain, thousands of people had turned out to welcome him to the city. The Lord Mayor told Lord Kitchener that the he was delighted to be enrolling his name as a Freeman of the City. They now had the proud honour of giving Lord Kitchener a true Yorkshire welcome.' (*The Times*)

OCTOBER 1ST

1836: A report of a quarrel which had taken place on Tuesday evening between an Italian musician, Joseph Ramasarte, and Eli Roebuck, a hackney coachman, in Furnival Street was published today. The Italian was said to have reached such a stage of aggravation that he stabbed Roebuck in the abdomen. It was said that Roebuck offered Ramasarte a sixpence to play another tune, but when he had done so, Roebuck refused to pay him, and struck him during an altercation that then broke out. Mrs Roebuck intervened and sent her husband to the stables of the Swan with Two Necks, but, as Roebuck was leaving the stables, Ramasarte stabbed him; the wound was so severe that the man's life was endangered. Information was given to the police and the watchmen, who were mustered for duty. One of them going to his beat along Pond Street had his attention drawn to a man who was being followed by a crowd of boys. He took Ramasarte into custody, and he was remanded in custody at the Town Hall by the magistrates on September 30th. Roebuck later went on to make a full recovery. (*Sheffield Independent*)

OCTOBER 2ND

1851: A report appeared in the local paper of Mr Henry Russell's production of *Far West* at the Theatre Royal, which drew full houses for the entirety of its run at the theatre. 'The first act consisted of a series of spirited scenes of the progress of the emigrant, commencing with his appearance onboard the ship, and concluding with his final settlement in the far west. The scene backdrops were well executed; with views of New York, the scenery of the North River, the falls of Niagara, the emigrant's first settlement and an American winter all proving to be remarkably beautiful. One in particular of the more humorous scenes illustrated the perils of settling too near to the river; astonishment befell upon the emigrant and his family one morning when they awoke to find their log hut moving slowly down a swollen river, which the audiences found very amusing. The second act of the play was devoted to unmasking the horrors of the slave trade. The cruelties perpetrated onboard the slaver's ships were truthfully depicted, and some excellent remarks were made by Mr Russell on the duty of all men to assist in putting a stop to the barbarity of the slave trade.' (*Sheffield Times*)

OCTOBER 3RD

1771: The anniversary of the Cutler's Feast fell upon this day, and, as was usually the case in these celebrations, some very important people had been invited. The Master Cutler, Mr William Trickett, had invited many noble guests, including the Dukes of Norfolk, Devonshire and Leeds, the Marquis of Rockingham, the Earl of Holderness and the Earl of Scarborough. Lords George and John Cavendish, the Earls of Effingham, Bute and Strafford and the Honourable John Manners, Lord John Murray and Sir George Saville were also in attendance. The Lord Mayor was on hand to greet the illustrious guests and welcome them to the feast. The Cutler's Feast traditionally was observed as a great holiday for the whole town of Sheffield, and the church bells were kept constantly ringing throughout the three days it lasted. Several booths and market stalls were erected in the church yard, High Street and Church Street for the sale of fruit, spices and so on, and for the whole three days all business was generally suspended in the town. Such a party atmosphere was reflected in the good sales that many of the pubs and beer houses made over the days of celebration of the trade on which Sheffield depends. (Batty, S.R., *Sheffield*, London, Ian Allen, 1984)

OCTOBER 4TH

1828: Today it was announced that the state of trade in Sheffield was deplorable, and a large volume of complaints from the tradesmen of the town were made. The *Sheffield Iris* states that: 'In the present state of the market in the East and West Indies and particular in America, the most spirited of our townsmen look but with a trembling hope towards those quarters, where they have heretofore found a vent for their goods. The larger mercantile establishments, whose heavy trans-Atlantic shipping orders used to be no sooner got up and sent off at the appointed season, than they began to recruit their warehouse stocks in the prospect of the returning periodical demands, are now apparently in a lethargic state. We by no means wish to insinuate from the remarks made with reference to the cutlery and edge tool manufacturers that the stagnation is universal, and that all business is at a stand. This of course is not the case; but the fact that a number of hands seeking work, and the greater numbers stinted in their earnings, leads us to the just conclusion that both masters and workmen in the staple branch of Sheffield trade are at this moment suffering to a great extent.' (*Sheffield Iris*)

OCTOBER 5TH

1869: It was reported today that a pork butcher, George Hillier of Percy Street, Neepsend Lane was brought back to Sheffield from Sedburgh, where he had been found having absconded after putting horse meat in pork sausages which were not fit for human consumption. It seems that the previous August, Hillier was in the habit of purchasing horse meat from John Young, who kept a knacker's yard on Pond Street. When asked by Young what he was using the meat for, he said it was for his master who trained dogs using the meat. Young, not satisfied with this explanation, informed Inspector Wood, who watched Hillier and ascertained who he was, and that he manufactured sausages at his premises on Percy Street. Hillier came into the knacker's yard one morning and purchased 35lbs of horse flesh, which he put into a basket and covered with a cloth. He was followed home by Inspector Wood and Mr Young, where they found the meat at his shop. He told them that he sold the sausages to people in the neighbourhood and begged leniency for the sake of his wife and children. Hillier was sentenced to six months' hard labour, the Bench stated they would have doubled the sentence if they could. (*Sheffield Times*)

OCTOBER 6TH

1870: A report was published detailing the visit of an Indian Prince, Prince Soliman Kudr, who was visiting Sheffield as the guest of the Master Cutler, W. Bragge Esq. 'His Highness the Nawab Nazim of Bengal arrived by the 6.40 p.m. train on October 5th, and, after being greeted by the Mayor and other officials, took up his quarters at Mr George Meyers' Victoria Station Hotel. His bright raiment's drew the attention of the crowd as he was transported in a carriage and the Prince seemed to be delighted to be here for the visit. He was scheduled to visit the house and grounds of Chatsworth, the seat of the Duke of Devonshire. His Royal Highness also expressed a considerable interest in the Oriental manuscripts, which were kept at Chatsworth. On October 7th, the Master Cutler has arranged for His Royal Highness and his party to visit several manufacturing works of the town. On Sunday, they will be the guests of Mr W. Bragge at the Cutler's Hall, where gifts will be exchanged. Mr Bragge has commissioned a fine set of cutlery for the Prince to take back with him to Bengal, and it is expected that their stay will be prolonged until the middle of next week.' (*Sheffield Independent*)

OCTOBER 7TH

1857: On this day, a letter was received and printed in a local newspaper which had come from a gentleman in Hyderabad, addressed to a relative in Sheffield. He states: 'My last letter may have produced some anxiety amongst you, which I should wish to remove as far as possible. We have thrown up fortifications around the Residency, and we could readily hold it against all comers, had danger only to be apprehended from without. We have had so many mournful instances of treachery among the native soldiers that we cannot but view them with distrust. This is the first day of a festival of Muharram, an annual festival among the Mussulman's which last ten days, and is not infrequently attended with tumult, from a vast assemblage of persons. An especial merit at this season is to evince their hatred of the "infidel" as they are pleased to term us. We have taken all the precautions in our power, but we are more safely situated than hundreds of our poor fellow countrymen in other parts of India, and it is horrible to think of the atrocities that have been committed at Cawnpore, Meerut, and Dehli. Four months from the present date, should see us well supplied with British troops and then follows fearful retribution.' (*Sheffield Independent*)

OCTOBER 8TH

1841: Today's newspaper revealed the atrocious state of the sanitary arrangements in Sheffield. A letter written to the editor of the *Sheffield Iris* stated: 'There is, and has been for a period of no less than twenty years, an intolerable nuisance of a shameful and injurious character, at the bottom of the Wicker. There is not a common sewer, to take away the sediments continually accumulating in the adjacent lanes. Walker Street, Andrew Lane and Wicker Lane, are never free from stagnant water, and filth of every description. The authorities of Brightside township have never tried to remedy the evil; but, at the present time, there is a favourable chance of effecting, at a little outlay, the object required, by throwing a common sewer into one which the Railway Company have made, I am certain that the ratepayers of Brightside will gladly endure higher rates in order that this menace can be remedied'. The *Sheffield Iris* comments that this was not the only letter on the same subject that had been received at the office. 'Several letters made comments which alluded to the same problem existing in other parts of the town and we hope that a committee may be formed to deal with such matters.' (*Sheffield Iris*)

OCTOBER 9TH

1851: It was announced today in the *Sheffield Times* that Sheffield was to have its own telegraph office. 'In a few weeks, the electric telegraph on the Manchester, Sheffield and Lincolnshire Railway is expected to be completed. The posts were already fixed from Manchester to below Gainsborough, and when everything was completed, Sheffield would be able to have telegraphic intelligence from Hull, the Irish Channel and the German Ocean conveyed in a few moments. Great excitement graced Sheffield's atmosphere for this technological innovation, which pleased manufacturers, men of business, as well as other bodies for its speed of delivery. Retford was to form the conveying point of communication with all parts of the kingdom, when the Great Northern Railway shall have closely connected the two great capitals, London and Edinburgh, and the station at Sheffield would consequently become a station of great importance. At the time, more than a hundred trains stopped there on a daily basis and with the increase of traffic upon the opening of the Great Northern Railway, the number would only increased. It seems that in the future many more people will have the opportunity to visit our great town.' (*Sheffield Times*)

OCTOBER 10TH

1835: On this day was held a meeting to hear a report which had been made by the Society for Bettering the Condition of the Poor in Sheffield. The report, which was in the form of questions and answers, revealed the state of the poor of the town. The findings stated: 'Many people are fully employed at this time and those who complain of want are generally the idle and intemperate. They do not send their children to schools regularly, preferring the Sunday school which is free. Children of nine or ten years might earn a shilling or eighteen pence a week to go towards food or rent. There are streets and alleys where both the dwellings and the inmates are notoriously dirty and the manners of young and old are correspondingly gross. Intemperance seems to have increased within late years, possibly due to the great number of beer houses and dram shops which have opened in every part of the town. The low prices frequently induce fathers and husbands to neglect their wives and children, for drunken companions. It is reported that scarcely one family in twenty regularly attend Divine Service yet there are many hundreds of families who keep holy His day.' (*Sheffield Iris*)

OCTOBER 11TH

1850: An account appeared in the newspapers on this day of two men called John Riley and Jacob Middleton who were arrested by night-watchman George King and charged with stealing a clock. It seems that about 10 p.m., Riley was seen walking towards the police station at the Town Hall with a clock in his hands. King asked him what he was doing and he made a statement to the effect that the clock had been stolen, and implicating Middleton as the guilty party. Margaret Hunter of New Meadow Street identified the clock as being hers, which had been stolen from her house between 6 p.m. and 8 p.m. that very evening. Riley stated that Middleton had gone to his house about 8.30 p.m., and asked for permission to leave the clock until the following morning. After Middleton had gone, he found out that a clock very similar to the one in his house had been stolen, and after enquiring about the character of Middleton and finding his address, he was then proceeding towards the Town Hall to give up the clock and inform the police, when he was arrested. Thankfully the police sergeant to whom he relayed this tale believed him; he sent two constables to arrest Middleton and Ridley was released. (*Yorkshire Post*)

OCTOBER 12TH

1844: On this day there was an article published about a sudden death at Wadsley, where the inquest had been held on Wednesday last. The inquest before coroner Mr T. Badger was held on the body of Mr William Smith Esq. of Wadsley Villa, aged sixty-six. The deceased gentleman had been with his daughter, who had left him at the church door with a lantern in his hand, to come home by a private road. When her father had not arrived home when expected, she sent a servant to seek him out, and, to her shock and horror, found him collapsed at the front door, with his lantern and hat a short distance off. He was lifted into the house and Mr Payne, the surgeon, was then sent for, but before he arrived Mr Smith had expired. Mrs Garforth, his daughter, told the coroner that her father had been in good spirits when she left him at the church and had not complained of any illness or pain, although he was depressed due to the death of her mother two years previously. The jury took just a little time before delivering a verdict of 'sudden but natural death'. (*Sheffield Iris*)

OCTOBER 13TH

1870: Today it was reported that a portion of the old ancient Manor Castle had fallen down. Built in 1516, it was the place where Mary Queen of Scots was kept whilst she was the prisoner of the Earl of Shrewsbury. Part of the castle was used as a beer house, known by the sign of the Norfolk Arms, occupied by Mr Knott. For some time, the middle portion of it had been deemed unsafe, and a chamber in it had not been used. The ground floor under the chamber was used as a bar. At 3 a.m. on the morning of October 13th, Mr Knott was awakened by a crash of falling brickwork, and, on getting out of his bedroom, he ascertained that the roof of the unsafe portion had fallen in. The weight of the stones which composed the roof broke through the floor of the middle room and all the debris fell into the bar. Nothing of any value was in the way and beyond the breaking of a few dishes, comparatively little damage was done. 'A portion of the roof over the kitchen adjoining the part that fell this morning looks very unsafe and fears were entertained that it would fall later today.' (*Sheffield Independent*)

OCTOBER 14TH

1892: Summonses against seven firms in Sheffield for the abatement of smoke nuisance were published in the local newspapers. The summonses were issued from the medical officer of health, Dr Harvey Littlejohn, who told the magistrates that a public meeting had been called to assess the smoke nuisance in Sheffield. The Health Committee had been told to 'apply all the means in their power to suppress the smoke nuisance' and it had been noted that once the committee had served notice on manufacturers that the emission of smoke fell to a remarkable extent. He told the magistrates that apparatus could be bought, which, when fixed on the chimney, would reduce the emissions. The first case was of a brewer in Rutland Road, who had on his premises a chimney which sent forth black smoke in such large quantities as to be a nuisance. The brewer informed the magistrate that he had bought the apparatus but he had not got it to work. The magistrate fined him £1 and gave him a week to reduce his emissions. The other firms were similarly dealt with and given fines ranging from £1 to £5. (*Sheffield Star*)

OCTOBER 15TH

1859: An extraordinary find at St John's Church was published in the newspapers on this day. 'It seems that a number of coffin plates and several coffins containing corpses had been found in an underground vault. The circumstances had given rise to a great anxiety on the part of families who already had relatives interred in the churchyard. The churchwardens had received several urgent demands to have graves opened up by relatives of the deceased concerned, in order to satisfy themselves that their graves had not been disturbed. Upon further investigation, it was found that this was impossible to do as no plan of the ground have been kept, which might have indicated where the different interment had taken place. The sexton had been removed from his post, and we understand that the churchwardens had been in communication with the Mayor with a view to having the matter fully investigated. We understand that the sexton's explanation about the corpses and coffins found in the vault was that they had not been interred at a sufficient depth in the first instance, and that he had taken them up for the purpose of re-interring them at a greater depth, but that some delay had occurred in doing so.' (*Sheffield Independent*)

OCTOBER 16TH

1819: 'Early in the morning of this day, two gamekeepers in the employ of Mr J.A.S. Wortley Esq. were completing their rounds at Wortley when they spotted four men who they suspected of poaching. They would have concealed themselves, but knew the men had already seen them. One of the gamekeepers went up to one of the gang he knew and said, 'Well my lad, have you got your gun with you this morning?' and he touched his waistcoat. The other man jumped back and exclaimed, 'Are you trying to rob me?' At the same time, he fired the gun, the contents passing completely through the keeper. Before the man had hit the ground, the three men attacked his companion, knocking him to the floor with the butt of the gun and beating him with sticks. He managed to get his own gun out of his pocket, and he shot at the group hitting one who fell to the floor. The other three ran off and the injured man crawled to a nearby cottage and gave the alarm. Warrants were issued and the man who shot the keeper was brought to Sheffield gaol, where he was told that the man was dead and he was therefore on a charge of murder.'(*Sheffield Iris*)

OCTOBER 17TH

1858: Today it was announced that the schoolchildren at the school run by Miss Shore of Meersbrook had been given a lovely treat by her the previous Thursday. It was her custom to treat the children once a year and it was reported that: 'According to the usual custom the children met at Meersbrook at 2 p.m. where they played running games until 4 p.m., when they were summoned to an abundant repast, rendered doubly grateful by their preliminary, innocent amusement. Play in the form of further games and tug of war was renewed until 7 p.m., at which hour they were again regaled with buns and milk. The children were kindly dismissed full of gratitude and loud in their praises of the lady whose hospitality they had partaken. Together with Mr Harrington Shore, Miss Shore had been untiring in her endeavours to please visitors. The weather being especially warm, there were many friends present, who seemed to enjoy themselves not a little in the hilarity and frolicsomeness of the young people.' The parents of the children also added their thanks to Miss Shore for the food and the entertainment. (*Sheffield Times*)

OCTOBER 18TH

1871: A meeting which had been held the previous night in the Council Hall was reported in today's newspapers. The meeting, which had been convened by the Mayor, was in order to set up a subscription fund in aid of the sufferers from the terrible fire in Chicago. He told the large congregation that, although Sheffield was largely interested in American trade, he did not think this was the main reason for this meeting. Their desire was to show sympathy with the American people in their sad calamity and to repay some of their kindness the nation had displayed when the English people were in troubled times. The Master Cutler proposed a resolution that: 'This meeting deeply sympathize with the American people in the loss of life and destruction of property, caused by the recent fires in the United States, and resolve that a subscription be opened at once for the purpose of raising a fund to aid the multitudes, who are suffering from those calamities.' Mr Mark Firth told the crowd that Mr G. Hadfield MP had sent a cheque for 200 guineas, and Earl Fitzwilliam had sent a cheque for £100.

The Chicago Fire referred to burnt from Sunday October 8th to Tuesday October 10th and 90,000 people were left homeless. (*Sheffield Independent*)

OCTOBER 19TH

1867: 'Mary Harrison (62) appeared in the court charged with keeping a disorderly house in Sheffield. In reply to the magistrate, Inspector Rodgers said that he had known the prisoner for twenty years and she had been known to the police for all that time. The character of the house she had kept had been very bad indeed, and she had been fined on at least two occasions. The house had been closed since the apprehension of the prisoner. Harrison, who was very much affected by the charge, begged the court to remember that she had already been in prison for more than three months on a similar charge. She had a grandson who would take her from Sheffield, and she promised that if she was liberated, she would never keep such a house again. The magistrate, on passing sentence, said that she had been the cause of the drop in public morality and the complaints about her house had been a nuisance to the police. Keeping in mind the three months imprisonment she had already had, they would sentence her to a further term of three months. The prisoner was weeping as she was led from the dock.' (*Sheffield Times*)

OCTOBER 20TH

1866: An inquest that was held on the death of sixty-six-year-old George Atkins, who had been found dead in a potato field on Monday night, was published on this day. 'The inquest was held before the coroner, Mr D. Wightman, at the Sheffield mortuary. The body had been found in a field which belonged to Mr Ashworth of Longley Hall, by whom he had been hired to pick potatoes in the same field. It seems that shortly before 4 p.m. on the day of his death, his wife asked him to get her some potatoes for their tea, and, taking a small knife with him, he went to do her bidding. When he did not return within twenty minutes his wife sent her two sons to go and look for their father. Taking a lantern, they went out, but it was over an hour later before his body was found. His wife told the coroner that her husband had been in good health and she was sure that there was no suspicion of foul play. A doctor, who went to see the body the following day, stated that in his opinion the cause of death was apoplexy. The jury took little time before returning a verdict and death from natural causes was recorded.' (*Sheffield Times*)

OCTOBER 21ST

1848: Today the *Sheffield Iris* reported on a foot race which had started at the Barracks Tavern on Monday. The report stated that, 'the spot is most eligible one for such sports, and there were almost one thousand people who had collected by 4 p.m. Mr E. Broadbent, the landlord, was elected as the referee and the prize was a gold repeater watch, valued as 12 guineas'. The reporter gives an outline of the several men and what their handicaps were, and pointed out that the man most likely to win was an Irish lad named Conway. At 4.30 p.m. the race started, and halfway through three of the men were racing 'neck and neck'. Their names were Conway, Frost and Holland. About 100 yards from the finishing line, Holland dropped out and left Conway and Frost energetically contending for the prize. After a great struggle, Conway won by a yard, amidst cheers from the crowd. The reporter stated that 'a fairer or better race had seldom been witnessed which had required about 25 turns around the track to run 5 miles'. Mr Broadbent stated that he was delighted to present the prize to Conway, who thanked him. (*Sheffield Iris*)

OCTOBER 22ND

1889: A report of a fatal accident, which had happened in 'an unfortunate household', was published in the *Sheffield Weekly Telegraph today*. 'On Sunday evening Sabina Stoddard (55), who lived on Montague Street, fell down some stairs. The deceased had recently become very infirm, and as a consequence of this, had been attended to by a woman named Harriett Isaacs. She was going upstairs when she fell and rolled to the bottom, where she was picked up by Isaacs and Florence Moseley, a domestic servant employed by Mr Stoddard. In her fall her head had doubled under her body and she had landed at the bottom in such a manner that the weight of her body was on her neck. Medical assistance was sent for, but having broken her neck she was dead before the surgeon arrived. The husband of the dead woman was recently injured in a railway accident at Hexthorpe and has never been in good health since. In addition to this misfortune, the deceased's daughter-in-law was murdered two years ago by a man named Hobson, and the servant Florence Moseley was stabbed on the same occasion and narrowly escaped being murdered too.' The reporter stated that he hoped that this would be an end to the family's misfortune. (*Sheffield Weekly Telegraph*)

OCTOBER 23RD

1861: A report appeared in the *Sheffield Times* about a soldier who had fired on civilians at Hollow Meadows on August 23rd of the same year. He had been remanded several times as the crime was being dealt with by the military authorities and not by the magistrates. 'The Sheffield Magistrates court yesterday discussed whether it would be correct to try the soldier again as a civilian crime. It seems that Michael Mason, a sergeant of the 58th Regiment, was sent off with several private soldiers from Sheffield to Manchester on escort duty. It was known that he was drunk and he fired a loaded rifle at civilians along the route and also at windows. The people who had been fired upon went to the barracks to complain and Col. Peabody rightly reported the affair to his commanding officer. It was agreed that he would be tried by Court Martial and he was found guilty and sentenced to twelve months in the prison at Weedon, with hard labour. It was also reported that he would also lose his rank and possibly his pension. The Sheffield Bench agreed that they could take the case no further as the man was already in prison and serving his sentence.' (*Sheffield Times*)

OCTOBER 24TH

1877: A report of a man who supposedly died from choking at a Sheffield eating house the previous evening was printed today. 'It seems that the man, Henry Scholey, a pork butcher, accompanied by two other men went to the eating house of Mr Williams on Furnival Road, for the purpose of having his dinner. He ordered pork chop and mashed potatoes, but it was noted that he was considerably the worse for drink and it was said that he had been drinking hard for almost a month or six weeks prior to his death. Soon after commencing his dinner, he was taken suddenly ill and was unable to speak, and could breathe only with the greatest difficulty. No medical man being at hand, it was considered best to remove him with all haste to the infirmary. This was done, but it is believed the man was dead before his arrival there. The deceased was about forty-five years of age. It was said that a small legacy and domestic trouble were the combined cause of his alcoholism. Whether choking was the cause of death, those speculating could only surmise; the full verdict could not be ascertained until a medical examination had been made. This was completed later on during this day.' (*Sheffield Post*)

OCTOBER 25TH

1917: General Smuts and Admiral Sir John Jellicoe received the Freedom of the City of Sheffield. The ceremony came at the end of a long and interesting round of visits to great armament works, on the 'smoke saturated outskirts of the city'. The previous night they had addressed a great war aims meeting in the spacious drill hall, which was attended by wounded soldiers. The demonstration of more than 6,000 people heard several stirring speeches as the audience, carried away with enthusiasm, called for a resolution, recording: 'Its inflexible determination to continue the war to a victorious end. We vow to continue the struggle in maintenance of those ideals of liberty and justice which are the common and sacred causes of the Allies.' Emphasis was made by General Smuts on the necessity of national unity and the danger of a 'negotiated peace' as he warned them that if this war is not won, the British Empire will not last. 'Militarism must be swept off the earth and permanent machinery established for the maintenance of peace.' (*The Times*)

OCTOBER 26TH

1833: On this night, the *Sheffield Iris* reported that: 'Twenty-six convicts, who were sentenced to transportation at the Sheffield Sessions, were chained two and two together ready for their removal tomorrow to Wakefield. Fourteen of these men were put into the first cell and twelve in another. During the night, six of them managed to execute their escape. As no force appeared to have been used on the lock or the door of the first cell, it was believed that they were never fully locked away in the cell in the first place, as the door was very new, heavy and difficult to open. When the prisoners went out into the yard, the man who had been putting rivets on their chains left his tool box behind by mistake. Returning back to the first cell, the prisoners broke open the lid and drew out a hammer with which to smash their irons. Out of the fourteen prisoners in the cell, six of them scaled a wall and dropped into Waingate. But the alarm was given, and the remaining eight were prevented from following their fellow prisoners. The constables were dispatched to search some of the haunts of the desperate characters of the town, but without success. Information was dispatched to other neighbourhoods however the men remained at large'. (*Sheffield Iris*)

OCTOBER 27TH

1821: The Burns Society of the town received a letter from the widow of the poet. A present of a silver candlestick and a tray and snuffers had been presented to her by a native of Dumfries, Mr Brown, who was also a Steward to the Burns Society. Sheffield poet James Montgomery had inscribed the tray with his own poem, which read:

> He passed thro life's tempestuous night,
> A brilliant trembling Northern light;
> Thro years to come he shines from afar,
> A fixed unsettling polar star.

Mrs Burns, writing from Dumfries on October 25th, thanked them for the present, stating that:

> I shall carefully preserve this interesting gift while I live, and when in the course of nature it passes into the possession of my children, I need not say that it will be equally prized. The value of this elegant gift is much enhanced by the tribute paid to the memory of my husband, from the pen of a poet not less celebrated for his talent than for his philanthropy. I also acknowledge my thanks to Mr Brown for the very handsome manner in which he presented this flattering mark of your attention.

Signed Gentlemen your gratefully obliged Jean Burns.

(*Sheffield Iris*)

OCTOBER 28TH

1838: 'A public meeting was held at Attercliffe on this day. The rate payers resolved unanimously not to pull down or to sell the parochial workhouse, or its furniture, feeling a conviction that the Poor Law Amendment Act would within twelve months be repealed and the management of the poor would once again be put back in the hands of the parishes. The meeting which was attended by hundreds of people on Attercliffe Common, universally condemned the diet table that the Poor Law Commissioners had agreed would be suitable fare for workhouse paupers in Sheffield. Several speakers instanced cases of lingering death of elderly people, being fed upon water, gruel and other meagre fare. They also criticised the assistant commissioner of the Poor Law who had ordered that tea, snuff, tobacco, sugar and other little articles, "the fruits of self deprivations on the part of poor relatives towards the paupers who offers to them as proof of affection" are to be taken from the wretched poor and thrown away. They resolved to write to the Poor Law Commissioners in London and register their protests against the Poor Law Amendment Act and strongly complain about the workhouse diets.' (*Sheffield Iris*)

OCTOBER 29TH

1839: Today was published an account of a child's death which was suspected to be murder. The previous Tuesday, a man and a woman carrying a newborn baby went to a pub called the Bay Horse and said that they wanted a wet nurse for the child. The bell man was accordingly sent out to give notice that a nurse was wanted, and, later the same day, a relative of the landlord, Mrs Walker, offered to take the child. The pair accompanied her to her house at Intake, and without her getting any details from the couple, they promised to come back on Saturday and bring extra clothes and to pay her. The next day, the child died. Suspicion was aroused by a servant girl at the Bay Horse who said that she had seen the woman give the baby something from a bottle. The coroner was informed and agreed to hold an inquest on Saturday. It appeared that the mother of the child was unmarried, and had the baby on Monday night; to keep the birth a secret, early the following morning the baby was brought to Sheffield. The couple were reprimanded by the coroner for taking the child out so early after birth, and a verdict of 'natural death' was recorded. (*Sheffield Independent*)

OCTOBER 30TH

1889: Some of the poor housing in Sheffield was described in a letter in the local newspaper from Jonathon Taylor, who was from an association anxious to do something to better the conditions in the houses of the poor. He describes a visit that he made to some houses in the centre of the town. In one house containing two rooms, described as 'one up and one down', he found 'a poor woman in bed in the upstairs room and rain water coming through the roof in six places. In another court, I found six pigs kept within about four feet of the pantry window and in the house was a man and his wife and eight children. In another street I spoke to an old gentleman who had lived in the same house since childhood. The house had no water and poor sanitation and cellars which flooded during wet weather. In another courtyard I found 12 houses in a very squalid condition and unfit for human habitation'. Taylor asks the editor, 'surely the landlords should be made to keep the houses in better condition'. He ends his letter by saying that, 'our association has a mission to enlighten the public to the conditions in which many people of the town exist'. (*Sheffield Star*)

OCTOBER 31ST

1892: A Young Man's Parlour was opened in connection with the Park Wesleyan Sunday School on Duke Street, by local MP Mr T.W. Ward. The object of the venture was to afford the young men connected with the school an opportunity of spending pleasant evenings together. The *Sheffield Journal* stated that: 'Simple games may be indulged in and periodicals are placed on the table and it is intended to form a library. The room is tastefully furnished and there is accommodation for about 22 persons. The room together with alterations in the two vestries has entailed a cost of about £50.' It appears that the Revd W. Cornelius Jones, the pastor of the Park Wesleyan Church, has had the management of the renovating of the parlour. The opening of the room was followed by an entertainment and a coffee supper. A piano solo and solos on the autoharp were given by Miss Lillian Frith. Songs were rendered by Mr A.J. Ward and Mr Rawson. A reading was given by Revd Cornelius Jones and a recitation by Mr J.G. Hyles. 'The concert was very much enjoyed and it is felt that many young men will find suitable entertainment within the parlour.' (*Sheffield Journal*)

NOVEMBER 1ST

1610: On this day, Robert Rollinson, a mercer of Sheffield, drew up an agreement with his tenants in Figtree Lane about rules for the use of the Plumtree Well, which he had sunk at his own cost for their joint use. In the agreement were provisions for making and keeping in good repair, a fence around the well with a door which could be locked at night, and it was found necessary to prohibit the washing of clothes and calfes [*sic*] heads in the well. All tenants were to pay a farthing a year for the privilege of this well. (Walton, M., *Sheffield: Its Story and its Achievements, Sheffield, Amethyst Press,* 1984)

———— ◆ ————

1900: Today it was announced that Winston Churchill was to deliver a lecture in the Albert Hall:

Albert Hall, Sheffield, beg to announce that Mr Winston Churchill will give his public lecture entitled 'The War as I saw it' on Friday, November 16th at 8 p.m. The Lecture will be illustrated by Lantern Slides from Photos. Doors open at 7.15 p.m.

Reserved Balcony and Stalls	4s
Saloon	2s 6d
Second Tier and Balcony	1s

Plan and tickets are on sale at Mr Peace's office, Albert Hall

(*Sheffield Independent*)

NOVEMBER 2ND

1874: A publican was fined for permitting drunkenness on his premises. William Guest, the landlord of the Turf Tavern, West Bar appeared before magistrates Alderman Brittain, Alderman Hunter and Mr H.J. Dixon yesterday. It seems that on October 21st, PC Chambers was on duty in Bridge Street and saw four men and two women in a state of intoxication. They went into Mr Chapman's house, who refused to serve them, and then went into the Turf Tavern. PC Mussenden then arrived and the two policemen entered the tavern, where they found the four men and two women with drinks before them. The officers called the attention of the landlord to the fact that the people were drunk. Guest stated that he didn't think they were, but he would take the drinks from them, but the officers told him that they would have to report the matter. His defence stated that he had not served them with the drinks and that the group had sat down at a table where drinks had been left, but the magistrates fined him £2 and costs and told him that if he was charged again with the same offence his license would be revoked. (*Sheffield Post*)

NOVEMBER 3RD

1853: This evening an inquest was held at Sheffield Infirmary on the death of George Needham (11), a fork grinder employed by John Sanderson at the Towel Wheel, Blonk Street. The previous Saturday he and two companions, Walter Burton (13) and James Sanderson (11), were alone in the 'hull'. An old bladder lay upon the wall on which the shaft worked about the height of four yards from the floor. The deceased had seen the bladder and climbed up to get it. The key of the box which couples the shaft protrudes a few inches. Whilst the deceased stood upon the wall, the key became entangled in his smock and he was whirled around several times by the shaft. When all his clothes were torn off he fell upon the ground. His right leg was fractured and he was much injured about the chest. He was removed and taken to the infirmary immediately, but died at 6 a.m. on the morning of November 2nd of shock sustained from his injuries. It was stated that Mr Sanderson rarely worked with the boys who are supervised by his seventeen-year-old son, and the coroner stated that it was improper that the boys should have been left unsupervised. The verdict was 'accidental death'. (*Sheffield Free Press*)

NOVEMBER 4TH

1861: The local newspapers on this day listed a specialty act which had become popular in Sheffield; albeit one which, in this generation, would not be deemed at politically correct. They were the Christy Minstrels, who were black-faced entertainers; a reporter described them as playing to packed audiences at the Music Hall this week. 'This ever popular company is composed of a large number of first class delineators of Negro life and character, and in this manner has obtained a great reputation. The songs and choruses are given with great effect and the instrumental music is really admirable. The burlesque opera – a great feature of the Christy entertainment – has lost none of its attraction, and the acting and singing are equally excellent. The dresses and the droll make-up of the performers are irresistibly ludicrous. The performance last night was received with great favour by the packed audiences and the demands for the repetition of favourite songs were numerous. The company will remain here for the rest of the week and we urge anyone who enjoys Christy songs and dance not to miss these irresistible performers.' After the original group (called the Christy Minstrels) disbanded in 1861, all entertainers of the same variety took on the name and travelled the provinces to great acclaim. (*Sheffield Times*)

November 5th

1850: Tonight saw the first of a two-evening literary and dramatic monologue by Mr Bunn, who delivered his talk in the large room of the Athenaeum and Mechanics Institute on Surrey Street. The *Sheffield Independent* reported that: 'He started by briefly sketching the career of Shakespeare, imparting additional interest to his remarks by a series of beautiful pictorial illustrations connected with the poet's life. The second part was of a more amusing character and consisted of a series of lively sketches of several of the most eminent men connected with the stage, accompanied by illustrations of the style of acting. Mr Bunn, in a very forceful manner, illustrated how a character in a tragedy may be made of a laughter-provoking nature, or endowed with malice or revenge. He also sketched the past, present and future prospects of the drama, expressing his belief that notwithstanding the dearth of tragedians of any eminence at the present time, there was a bright future for many new actors emerging then. His power of mimicry was superb as he closed the evening with a scene from the witches of 'Macbeth' and also a drunken sailor from the 'Tempest'. We understand that tomorrow night's programme will continue on this theme.' (*Sheffield Independent*)

NOVEMBER 6TH

1863: An inquest was held on the fifty-nine victims of the Edmunds Main Colliery explosion, which had occurred almost a year previously. Rather than hold fifty-nine individual inquests, it was agreed that just one miner would be the subject of the inquest. The matter had been fully examined and the verdict was that James Ellis came to his death by suffocation, caused by an explosion of gas on Monday, 8th December 1862. Whilst summing up for the jury the coroner stated that: 'We are of the opinion that the explosion was owing to the dangerous use of gunpowder in blasting the coal in the dip board gate at this mine. The practice of blasting ought not to have been permitted by the managers, or prosecuted by the workmen after the system of wedging had been introduced'.

A further inquest had been held December 23rd 1862 following the death of two men named Davy and Pickering at the same colliery. After hearing the statements of many witnesses a verdict of 'accidental death' was brought in by the jury. The coroner once again censured the management of the pit and requested that safer methods be used in blasting in the mines. (*Sheffield Times*)

NOVEMBER 7TH

1840: A caution was printed in today's edition of the *Sheffield Times*, regarding a fraudulent firm from Glasgow who were flooding Sheffield with orders. The report stated that: 'We are required to caution the merchants and manufacturers of Sheffield against receiving and executing orders from a certain firm in Glasgow without making some enquiries first. A few days ago a respectable house in this town received an order from the firm in question, for goods, and, not being known to the parties, the latter gave a reference to another establishment. Our townsman very prudently before they attended to the favours of their northern customers, or their "respectable reference" made application elsewhere, and discovered that both the Glasgow firm and the parties they referred to were a joint stock swindling concern. Thinking it probable that other merchants may be honoured with similar commands from the same company, we advise them to be equally cautious as their neighbours, and not to be duped out of their property by such swindling scoundrels'. The reporter ended his account by apologising for the fact that 'the law of libel prevents our giving the names of the joint stock cheats for their characters deserve the fullest exposure'. (*Sheffield Times*)

NOVEMBER 8TH

1530: Cardinal Wolsey arrives in Sheffield, en route to London to take his trial for treason. Whilst at the Manor Lodge he spent eighteen days as a prisoner of the Earl of Shrewsbury, who treated him as an equal despite the fact that he was a prisoner. His fall from grace was very unpopular with the people, who lined the route into Sheffield crying out 'God Save your Grace'. He fell ill three days later at Leicester and there he died and was buried in the Lady Chapel of the Abbey. (Hey, D., *A History of Sheffield*, Carnegie Publishing, 1998)

* * *

1895: The Duke of Devonshire visited Sheffield on this day, where he inspected seven industries and had lunch at the Cutler's Hall. The Duke expressed the pleasure with which he had seen the immense variations of the application for which iron and steel could be used in different processes in Sheffield. He told the Master Cutler: the city was perhaps more interesting to him still as a member of the Government than it could be to a private individual, 'for Sheffield was the centre on which the Government must depend for the provision of material which it is necessary for the defensive and offensive armaments of war'. He then concluded by proposing the health of the Master Cutler. (*The Times*)

NOVEMBER 9TH

1874: A remarkable and impudent burglary took place in Fernley Place. The *Sheffield Post* today reported that: 'The house was occupied by Mr S. Barnsley and while it was left today for just a few hours, the house was entered and ransacked. The thieves made their entrance through a window at the back of the house, which was presumably left unfastened. To do this they had to climb over a wall, and it is estimated that they made use of a ladder left nearby. They ransacked the house, leaving the bedrooms in the most disorder. In their attempts to open a chest of drawers, some of them being locked, they simply wrenched off the top of the drawers. It is believed that the burglar's favourite instrument "the jemmy" was used for this purpose. With the top off, the access to the drawers was an easy matter. Two watches and chains were left on one of the bedside cabinets and were recovered by the owner. This indicates that they must have been disturbed before they had time to finish their operation. The idea is strengthened by the fact that they overlooked a child's money box containing twenty-five shillings, whilst they took away two pence which had been left on a shelf.' (*Sheffield Post*)

NOVEMBER 10TH

1846: An inquest was held on death of twenty-eight-year-old Sarah Grace on this day at the Sheffield Workhouse. She had lived in a court in Bailey Fields and had made a livelihood out of binding boots and shoes. On Thursday, a neighbour had been in the yard when she rapped on the window. Entering the house she found Sarah very ill, and, despite obtaining medicine from the Dispensary, she continued to grow worse until Monday, when she went for a girl of bad character named Ann Goodlad, who had been her companion. Goodlad found her in a deplorable state and took her to the workhouse in a cab. She then received every attention both from the matron and the medical officer, but was so rapidly sinking that it was not expected that she would recover, and she died at 6 a.m. the next morning. The house she had lived in was filthy and completely without furniture. In the lower room was only a table and two chairs and the bedroom contained a mattress on the floor in one corner and a heap of straw in the other, which together formed her bed. There were no blankets or any coverings for the bed found in the house. (*Sheffield Times*)

NOVEMBER 11TH

1847: Today's newspapers called for a Worker's Institute to be opened in Sheffield. Councillor Ironside chaired the meeting, which was mainly comprised of working classes. He told them that: 'It was well known that the workers were kept so much to their labour that they had little time to study. It is important that people had knowledge to guide their power. The working men of Sheffield had now begun to find that power and to use it. He believed that they should take matters into their own hands, and it was for that reason that he hailed the idea of a Workers Institution'. Mr Ironside proceeded to read the plan, which stated that it was the purpose to furnish a good education by the simplest and most effective method at a price, which should simply pay the expenses. The mode of government should be a committee of twelve, elected at half-year meetings, who should meet once a month and keep minutes of their proceedings. At their first meeting they should elect a president, a treasurer and a secretary and plan the evening meetings and the subjects they were to teach. Councillor Payne agreed that the plan be adopted and that a subscription be started to establish a Workers Institute as soon as possible. (*Sheffield Iris*)

November 12th

1296: On this day, the Lord of the Manor of Sheffield, Thomas de Furnival, obtained a Royal Charter which allowed the holding of a market every Tuesday and of a fair on the Eve Feast, and on the morrow of Holy Trinity (a moveable feast in May or June). At the same time he obtained another Charter which formalized his right to hunt in his own park, and shortly afterwards he granted his townsmen another Charter confirming their privileges, which had long been held by right. He had previously had justification to claim himself as a Lord, questioned by a group of Commissioners in 1281. He had replied that the right to administer capital punishment, to hunt and to hold fairs and markets, and to have a windmill and to regulate the weight and price of bread had been held by his ancestors since time immemorial. This enquiry gives us the first evidence that a market had long been held at Sheffield for many years. It seems that by obtaining these Charters he was concerned to get everything down in writing, instead of relying on oral memory, as had done in the past. (Hey, D., *A History of Sheffield*, Carnegie Publishing, 1998)

November 13th

1830: It was noted today in the *Sheffield Independent* that: 'Now the darker nights are here again, there had been several reports of a number of active and stout lads who are practicing the activities of highwaymen, and waylaying respectable persons returning to their homes late at night. They are usually observed in parties of two or three, generally provided with sticks and particularly frequent the road between Sheffield and Rotherham. They usually select aged persons or those encumbered with baskets, and after knocking the person down, run off with any property they can seize. Two such young men, Charles Ellis and Robert Hyde, were captured after knocking down Mr Badger in Rotherham and brought back to Sheffield. On Monday last, they were examined by the magistrate, Dr Milner, and given three months imprisonment at the Wakefield House of Correction. He also warned people who travelled at night to make sure that they had a companion with them on their journey home. Ellis who is about 16 years of age, in order to try to have a lesser prison sentence, also named four or five boys of the same character and age as himself as other members of the gang.' (*Sheffield Independent*)

NOVEMBER 14TH

1855: Today there appeared a report concerning the Hyde Park Riots in the *Sheffield Free Press*. At the Middlesex Sessions, an appeal had been made by Mr John Bradley, a bookseller, against a conviction by a police magistrate for unlawfully inciting diverse persons to resist one John Bickerson. He was an Inspector of Police in the execution of his duty in Hyde Park in London. The riots were a result of the condemnation of the Sunday Trading Bill when a mob of 150,000 assembled in Hyde Park to protest. The Bill prohibited the sale of beer on Sundays between 2 p.m. and 6 p.m. and after 10 p.m. and it was very unpopular. Mr Bradley was engaged in distributing handbills headed 'Betrayal of England' and stating 'the particulars of the crimes of the government' which had been published in the Free Press at their offices on Angel Street, Sheffield. Bickerson had arrested Bradley and brought him before the magistrates, where he was fined 61s, or given the option of a fourteen days' imprisonment. The assistant judge said that it did not appear that Bradley had any other object other than to promote the sale of the newspaper and it was not intended to incite resistance to the police authorities, and the conviction was therefore quashed. (*Sheffield Free Press*)

NOVEMBER 15TH

1850: An accident occurred this morning on the Manchester, Sheffield and Lincolnshire Railway in the vicinity of the Sheffield station, in which a man named Charles Gray of Harvest Lane sustained serious injuries. The *Yorkshire Post* reported that: 'It appears that Gray, who had been employed by the coal merchant Mr France, was engaged in arranging some coal wagons on the side near the aqueduct, when an unattached engine passed him. Gray immediately ran after it in order to have a ride. Having come up to the engine, he was cautioned by the fireman, who considered it was going at too rapid a speed to allow his doing so with safety. Gray, however, disregarded the caution and was punished for his temerity. He had placed his foot on the step and was raising himself up when he fell forward with one leg partially lying on the rails. The engine wheels caught his heel, the calf of the leg and thigh, tearing the flesh to a frightful extent. The man was immediately removed home where he was attended by a surgeon, Mr Reedal, who advised his removal to the Infirmary without delay. This was accomplished and where we understand he is making steady progress.' (*Yorkshire Post*)

November 16th

1829: On this day, it was reported that there was a fox chase in the centre of Sheffield. 'About 9 a.m. the population heard shouts at the bottom of Rockingham, and the inhabitants of the neighbourhood were animated in consequence of the fine fox making his appearance. Reynard crossed South Street of Messrs Alsopp's workshop and quickly turned along a back lane and through a passage to South Street. Once again, nearly opposite the chapel, he ran down a lane where he was hotly pursued. Large crowds started to gather, as he passed the new market in gallant style, and fled down one of the streets leading to Porter Street. He then headed towards a vacant piece of ground near Eyre Street, where his pursuers captured him with the loss of one his hind feet and within a few hundred yards of where he first started. Amidst the shouts and acclamations of a vast number of men, women and children who had collected together during this extraordinary chase, with sticks, pokers and almost every description of weapons upon which they could hastily lay their hands. He was carried alive by the tail into Mr Jessop's Yard, where he was quickly dispatched.' (*Sheffield Courant*)

NOVEMBER 17TH

1856: Tonight the members of the Sheffield Sacred Harmonic Society gave their first performance for the season. The newspaper on the following day gave it a terrible review stating that: 'We very highly approve for "music for the people" and are very unwilling to find fault with so laudable an attempt to provide cheap, rational amusement for the masses, but as music critics, we must protest against the production of great works in so imperfect a condition as was the performance of "Samson" last night. To spoil the masterpieces of Handel is not the way to make an audience love music. Instruments untuned, voices untrained, sopranos inaudible, a style of conducting equally exaggerated and ineffective, all combine to make a performance far below the point of merit where criticism might be supposed to begin its work'. The paper also pointed out that these concerts were becoming more expensive as originally tickets had been offered at 1s, 6d and 3d but these tickets had now doubled in price. In conclusion the reporter noted that, 'We would suggest that a firmer hand and a truer ear are required for the correct interpretation of Handel than appears to rule over this society'. (*Sheffield Independent*)

November 18th

1821: The accounts of the Sheffield and Hallamshire Savings Bank were announced in today's newspapers: 'We understand the sum now expended in debentures bearing interest amounts to £11,000 and that 590 accounts have now been opened. We are strenuous advocates for these popular institutions, which are well calculated, not only to benefit the parties who invest their property therein in a pecuniary point of view, but to train them to habits of industry and prudence in order to improve the moral condition of the lower classes of the community. We conceive it therefore to be our duty at this time to impress upon the labouring and industrious classes (and more particularly those whose situations enable them to lay aside a portion of their earnings) the duty of making provision for future wants. Let them remember that sickness is not the only misfortune that awaits the poor, but that the virtuous and industrious are sometimes reduced to distress for want of employment. How great then will be the satisfaction they experience, that the earnings of their honest industry have not been wasted in dissipation. They will be enabled when poverty presses upon them, to reap the rewards of their virtuous and frugal habits; a satisfaction which the idle will never know'. (*Sheffield Independent*)

NOVEMBER 19TH

1863: Today it was reported that a local townsman named Mr William White Junior, of Fulwood Parsonage, has for the last two years been engaged in compiling a history of the county of Norfolk to which the Prince of Wales some time ago gave his patronage. The *Sheffield Times* reported that: 'We understand that he has just received the following acknowledgement from his Royal Highness of the receipt of the handsome bound copy of the first part of the work:

Sandringham, Kings Lynn, 16th November 1863

Sir,
I am desired by the Prince of Wales to thank you for your kindness in sending to him your work on the botany, geology and ornithology of Norfolk, which his Royal Highness has pleasure in accepting. He has asked me to pass on his thanks for this most commendable study.

I am Sir, your most obedient servant
HERBERT FISHER

It is hoped that the second part of this work will be completed some time next year. Mr William White told our reporter that he was very gratified to receive the letter from the Prince of Wales.' (*Sheffield Times*)

NOVEMBER 20TH

1859: A case was reported today which had been brought before the magistrates of a man named Henry Milner, who had opened a beer house on West Bar Green and, according to the police authorities, had a conviction for a felony. An Act of Parliament stated that no person with a conviction can open a beerhouse. When he came to court, the chief constable told the bench that not only had Milner been convicted of felony three times, but also the house had not been conducted properly. The first conviction had been in 1849, when Sergeant Greenhough proved that he had witnessed the man selling beer. His defence, Mr Turner, admitted that his client had broken the law, but urged in mitigation that Milner now worked for a respectable firm, and that because he had once fallen, he should not to be prevented from getting an honest livelihood. The reason for the Act was because that business afforded them a greater facility as an inducement to get into their old ways again. Mr Turner stated that the justice of the case would be met if the defendant consented to close the house. Milner was fined 5s and costs and told to close the house within a week. (*Daily Telegraph*)

November 21st

1858: Today's newspaper contains an account of an extraordinary incident. 'Mr T. Colley, the landlord of the Bluebell Inn, was in the middle of a days shoot on the Duke of Norfolk's moor. A gamekeeper handed him a gun and pointed to a wild duck on one of the lakes as a target. Mr Colley went up a rising piece of ground in order to get a better shot. The duck appeared to have risen, and, just as he fired, something appeared to leap out of the lake and was shot. On it being obtained, it proved to be a large pike. But this was not all, for in firing Mr Colley was knocked backwards by the rebound of the gun, which knocked him over and he rolled down the hill. He was so stunned that he had to be lifted to his feet by his friends, and in doing so found that he had crushed a hare to death and had thus made one of the most extraordinary shots ever recorded. The duck, the pike and the hare have been stuffed and placed in a box, which is at present on show at the Bluebell Inn. The Duke of Norfolk, on hearing the story, sent Mr Colley a brace of grouse'. (*Sheffield Times*)

November 22nd

1842: It was reported today that a caesarean operation had been performed on twenty-six-year-old Sarah Booth, residing in Harvest Lane, from which effects she died a week later. This was her third child and the operation was performed by surgeon Mr W. Jackson in exactly four minutes. It was deemed that the operation was necessary due to a rupture of the uterus during childbirth. The *Sheffield Independent* stated that she 'underwent the operation with great fortitude. It is probable from her sinking condition at the time, that had the operation not been undertaken, death would have supervened in a few hours, as usually happens in such cases. During her first four of five days after the operation, there were circumstances leading her medical attendants to hope her constitution would surmount the tremendous injury which resulted from the rupture of the uterus. On the sixth day, the powers of nature evidently appeared to be giving way: on the seventh at two o' clock she died. Messrs Pearson, Gillatt and Clarke, surgeons, assisted Mr Jackson in this case. Fortunately for the sex that is subject to such cases, they are extremely rare. It is probable that there have been just 25 such cases in this country to date.' (*Sheffield Independent*)

NOVEMBER 23RD

1823: In the early hours of this morning, between 4 a.m. and 5 a.m., four villains attempted the premises of Mr Butterill on Shalesmoor. The *Yorkshire Post* reported that: 'They had succeeded to wrench from its hinges and bolts the shop door (leaving it a complete wreck) and to gain easy ingress, two of the gang watched without, while the other two were commencing the work of plunder within. Fortunately a neighbour, who was sitting up with a sick member of his family, overhearing a strange noise, threw up the sash, and gave the alarm; the crew instantly decamped, disappointed of any booty. The previous evening what was thought as the same gang had entered the house of Mr James at Hillfoot Bridge by means of a picklock and numerous valuable articles taken away. Rooms were ransacked both upstairs and downstairs. To aid their search, the gang had used newspapers as a torch, the dying embers of which were found on the carpet. The house itself had a narrow escape of being set on fire. It is thought by local police that the same gang has been operating in the area for many months now.' The reporter recommended that severer sentences for such criminals should be issued as a deterrent to further crimes. (*Yorkshire Post*)

NOVEMBER 24TH

1825: It was announced today that typhus fever 'is very general at present in Sheffield and the surrounding neighbourhood. Several fatal cases have been brought to the attention of the medical authorities just this very week. One of particular distress has occurred in the town and the case is not dissimilar to others heard about the town. It seemed that a person by the name of Robinson, a table knife cutler who resided in Broad Lane, was attacked with typhus fever, which was communicated from his wife. The poor woman died last Sunday and her husband on the following day. They were in one bed when she died. He was removed to a bed on the floor, where he witnessed his partner being placed in her coffin on Monday morning. He was afterwards placed back into the bed in which she had been so recently removed and he expired in it the same evening. The fatal cause of her illness was due to the devoted attention of a mother to a beloved son, who survives the effects on this same fever. Nine children were then left in the most distressing situation and the reporter asked that we bring these cases to your attention for any humane person who is able to offer help'. (*Sheffield Iris*)

NOVEMBER 25TH

1843: In today's *Sheffield Courant*, a letter from surgeon Mr John Nicholson was printed about the 'mad house' at the Attercliffe workhouse. Described as 'a damp place with low rooms and two confined courts, where little of the sky can be seen', the house was under the care of the master and matron and the medical officer, who only attended the property on three days of the week. The master, in the absence of the medical officer, could order any restraints in any case he thought fit. The number of lunatics was between twenty and thirty and they slept in overcrowded apartments, two to a bed. Mr Nicholson mentions the case of Aaron Parkin, a patient of whom he had attended due to his state of mind. He was mindful of the 'mad house' and wanted him to go to Wakefield Asylum, but in his absence Parkin was admitted to Attercliffe, where he got progressively worse before he was finally admitted to Wakefield. The aim of the letter was to draw the attention of the workhouse authorities to the management of such a disreputable place as Attercliffe. He requested 'the redress of its flagrant abuses, or what would be much better, its total abolition'. (*Sheffield Courant*)

NOVEMBER 26TH

1896: Today saw the opening of the selling of shares for the Sheffield and District Railway Company. The stock was valued at £400,000 and there were 40,000 shares available at £10 each. The London and Midland Bank of the Cornhill, Sheffield were commissioned to sell 35,000 shares (the remaining 5,000 would be reserved for the Great Eastern Railway Company). Interest would be paid to investors of 3 per cent per annum. The *Daily Telegraph* reported that: 'The railway, which was authorised by an Act of Parliament passed on 14 August 1896, is a short line of only 9½ miles in length which runs from Beighton in Derbyshire to a good station at Attercliffe. It thus creates a new and independent access for the Great Northern, the Great Eastern and the Lancashire Derbyshire and East Coast Railways to the City of Sheffield. The consumption of coal in and around Sheffield is very large both for domestic use and the use of the many iron and steelworks of the city. In addition, plated steel and cutlery which are the main trades of Sheffield combined with the great tonnage in and out of the iron and steel works is enormous. The whole of the trade manufacturers of Attercliffe signed the petition to Parliament for the Bill and gave evidence in support of it.' (*Daily Telgraph*)

NOVEMBER 27TH

1855: An inquest was held on the death of forty-one-year-old Hannah Finningley today, who died on 25 November of typhus fever whilst being treated by a 'quack doctor'. She had lived in a cluster of cottages at Upper Hallam with her husband. It was reported that 'the sanitary arrangements of the cottages were bad and neglected and no provision had been made to carry away the drainage and the refuse'. Mrs Finningley was attacked with fever three weeks before her death and her husband called in Mr Fox, a medical botanist. Revd C.E. Coombe visited and found the woman to be in a wretched state and called in Mr Wilson, the medical officer of the workhouse, who prescribed for her. Her husband, having more faith in medical botany, refused to comply with Mr Wilson's directions and continued to give her the herbal medicine prescribed by Mr Fox. As a consequence, after she died, the matter was brought to the attention of the coroner. Mr Fox gave evidence that he had successfully treated hundreds of people suffering from the same symptoms as Mrs Finningley. The inquest jury, after hearing all the evidence and examining the body, which had been placed in a coffin, returned a verdict that she had died of typhus fever. (*Sheffield Free Press*)

NOVEMBER 28TH

1858: An account was printed today of a daring house robbery, in which £95 was stolen. Mr Sterling Howard of Pitsmoor sat reading in the front room of his house after tea, and in the other room his father was playing the violin. The servants were going about their household duties about 8.30 p.m., when one of them went upstairs, where she was surprised to see a strange man coming out of Mr Howard's bedroom and proceed across the landing into a smaller room, which was above the portico of the front door. She raised the alarm and Mr Howard went upstairs into the room indicated by the servant girl, to find the man gone and the window open. It seems that the burglar had jumped onto the portico and then down onto the ground to make his escape. When investigations were made, it appeared that he had affected an entrance by climbing up one of the pillars of the portico whilst the family were at tea, in the lower back dining room. 'There was reason to fear that this audacious burglar will in all probability escape detection, as he was seen by no one except the servant, and by her for only a moment.' (*Sheffield Post*)

November 29th

1823: 'The fair at Sheffield commenced today and brought with it the usual depredations on the pockets of visitors. A popular part of the fair was the usual freak show and this year included a group of Eskimos. Their arrival yesterday was received with great interest in the town, and the queues lining up to see them this morning were vast. Crowds of people from every class queued up for almost an hour anxious to see these travellers from afar. They were said to exhibit a great variety of curiosities connected with their manners and customs, all of which are well worthy of inspection. There was a better show of horses this year than has been exhibited for many years; particularly of those calculated for draught. The supply of stock generally was good and sold freely at advanced prices. The year of 1823 saw a shortage of hogs, that were very much in demand. The price for Derby thin cheese was 63s – 70s and firm dairy cheeses were as high as 75s.' (*Yorkshire Post*)

NOVEMBER 30TH

1831: 'On this day several churches and Episcopal chapels in this parish were open for public worship to afford the inhabitants an opportunity for special prayer and humiliation. This was in the hope that God would be pleased to avert from this country that dreadful scourge Cholera Morbis. The services on the whole were better attended than might have been expected considering that different shops in the town were not closed. Liberal collections were made on the occasion to assist in defraying the expenses incurred by the Provisional Committee in the event of prevention or mitigation of the disease'. (*Sheffield Courant*)

———•◆•———

1863: The Lords of the Admiralty entered into a contract today with Messrs J. Brown and Co. of Sheffield for the supply of upwards of 1,000 tons of armour plating for the iron-cased frigate *Lord Warden* at Chatham. 'The armour plates are 5½ inches thick for her lower broadside tiers and the remainder 4½ inches thickness for the remainder. In this the *Lord Warden* differs from other armour-plated frigates as they are usually of the same thickness throughout. Having obtained this order it is thought that the men employed at Messrs Brown and Co. will be busily engaged for some time to come.' (*Sheffield Independent*)

DECEMBER IST

1855: The *Sheffield Times* today reported on a dinner which had been given to the workmen of Messrs John Wilson & Son of Sheffield. Described as a 'substantial dinner' which had been given last Saturday, accompanied by a 'liberal dessert' to the clerks and workmen of the company, the meal was eaten at the Spread Eagle Hotel on Fargate on the occasion of a first-class medal being awarded to the firm at the Paris Exhibition. To celebrate, the director of the company, George Wilson Esq., presided over the dinner and Mr Ridgeway, the manager of the works, occupied the vice chair. It was reported that: 'In the course of the evening, a variety of loyal and other toasts were proposed and duly responded to, and several congratulatory addresses were made. The whole of the evening was spent with great jollity and laughter between both employer and employees. There was little doubt that such celebrations can only foster a good working relationship which would reduce strife and ill will. It was said that Mr George Wilson always treated his workmen and office staff with respect and confidence. The proceedings throughout were characterized by the greatest unanimity and good will, and the testimony they bore to his invariable urbanity and kindness'. (*Sheffield Times*)

DECEMBER 2ND

1931: A meeting was held this afternoon in the Town Council chamber to discuss the difficulties encountered in the administration of the Means Test in Sheffield, and it was agreed to temporarily suspend it for the time being. It was maintained that: 'There were many anomalies in the test, and the Public Assistance Committee considered the position so unsatisfactory that they recommended the City Council to authorize its suspension until more enquiries had been made into the regulations relating to transitional payments. The Mayor stated that this might result in Public Assistance Commissioners being sent to Sheffield to take the work out of the hands of public representatives, but all parties agreed that there was a need for immediate instructions on the duties of the Public Assistance Committee. The council decided to send a deputation on the following day to London in order to interview the Minister of Labour and to discuss the matter and try to establish some kind of resolution. In the meantime, it was agreed to discontinue the imposition of the Means Test until the deputation returns. The Public Assistance Committee was asked to monitor the problem until they heard from the Minister of Labour'. (*The Times*)

DECEMBER 3RD

1882: On this day, an inquest was held at the Albion Inn, Sylvester Street on the death of fifty-year-old Emily Pool (50), whose body had been found floating in the river the day before. The *Sheffield Independent* reported that: 'The coroner was told that Emily had been suffering from epileptic fits for the last twenty years, although they had become more severe lately. On the day before her death, she had several fits, but appeared to be better later in the evening. She had gone out to the Newfield Inn for some beer, taking a pitcher with her. When she did not return Mrs Watkinson, who lodged with her, went to look for her, only to be told that she had not been seen at the inn. When her husband returned home from work, he also went out to look for her, but to no avail. In the early hours of this morning, her body was found floating face down, with her dress entangled in a piece of iron. The water at that spot was about four feet deep, whilst in other places it was only a matter of inches. Her husband gave his opinion that she had fallen in the water, after suffering from a fit. The jury returned the verdict of "found drowned".'(*Sheffield Independent*)

DECEMBER 4TH

1864: Today saw the first conviction under the new Game Act, when a poverty-struck young fellow named James Oxley was charged with having rabbits and nets unlawfully in his possession. The man had been arrested by a constable named Knight. He stated that he met the prisoner in Bramall Lane about 4.30 a.m. and noticed his pockets were bulky. He proceeded to search him and found six dead rabbits and four live ones in his pockets, as well as two nets. He took the prisoner to the Town Hall, where Oxley admitted that he was guilty of taking the rabbits in order to provide food for his wife and three children. He told the constable that the only reason he had taken the rabbits was because they were starving due to him being out of work. The Bench showed little sympathy as they fined him £5 and the court costs. As it was ridiculous to expect him to pay, he was therefore sentenced in default to two months' imprisonment. The Bench ordered that his nets be destroyed and the rabbits sold for the benefit of the Borough fund. (*Sheffield Times*)

DECEMBER 5TH

1851: An inquest was held this evening on the death of Edward Woodhead, who died in the house of a neighbour of his wife's the previous night. He had discharged himself from the Infirmary against the wishes of Mr Law, the house surgeon, to go home to die, but his wife refused to allow him to enter the house. This unfeeling woman refused to listen to his entreaties to allow him a night's lodgings, even when he promised to go to the workhouse the following day. He had been suffering from a pulmonary disease of the lung and knew that he wouldn't last much longer. Thankfully, a neighbour of his wife's took pity on the man and took him into her house, where he died a few hours later. The wife was charged with being the primary cause of her husband's death and an inquiry was held. She told the coroner and the jury that her husband had been an inveterate laudanum drinker and the surgeon who undertook the post-mortem confirmed this, having found his lungs much diseased through this habit. Nevertheless, the coroner castigated the woman and the jury brought a verdict of death produced by the effects of laudanum. (*Sheffield Independent*)

DECEMBER 6TH

1848: The *Sheffield Times* today reported on a woman's 'unfortunate mistake'. 'The chief constable, Mr Raynor, was returning from a meeting of the Health Committee at 6 p.m. last night, when he was accosted by a pretty young woman in the High Street. Catching hold of his coat, she asked him in the most endearing terms if she could accompany him. Mr Raynor gallantly acquiesced in the desire of his fair companion and the two proceeded lovingly together in the direction of the Town Hall. When they got as far as Angel Street the lady, disliking the way, turned into a shop and refused to proceed any further. When the shopkeeper recognised Mr Raynor and accidentally alerted his companion to his name and his profession, she let forth with a stream of abuse which tripped off her tongue. Mr Raynor left his fair companion and, arriving at the Town Hall, sent two constables to fetch her in and they found her in the company of a notorious prostitute in Angel Street. This morning the prisoner, who stated that she came from Manchester, was brought before the magistrates and she begged to be let off, but Mr Raynor pressed for a conviction and she was committed as a disorderly prostitute for 21 days. (*Sheffield Times*)

DECEMBER 7TH

1844: This morning, a private of the 8th Regiment of Foot named Benjamin Webster was brought before the Sheffield Magistrates Court and placed at the Bar. He had been brought into custody the night before and was charged with stealing a hat from a public house. A sergeant of the same regiment had also made enquiries into the case, and spoken to some of his companions from the previous night. He appeared before the magistrate to relate the incident. It seems that Webster had been drinking with several companions from the same regiment at the Globe Inn, Jessop Street, and someone in the party made a suggestion that they all exchange hats. To sounds of great hilarity, all the hats were exchanged, but a row ensued when one of the hats was lost. The other party charged the prisoner with having stolen it. In mitigation, the sergeant told the court that all the parties were tipsy together, and that since then the missing hat had been found under the table at the pub. The prisoner was discharged from the court on the promise that the sergeant would report him to the military authorities as being drunk. The sergeant agreed and the prisoner was discharged. (*Sheffield Independent*)

DECEMBER 8TH

1880: Today saw the death of a young man aged just twenty-seven at the Victoria Station in Sheffield from heart disease. His named was thought to be Mr F.A. Jolly and he arrived in Sheffield at noon, getting out of the Grimsby train. The *Evening Star* reported that: 'After being observed wandering around the platforms, seemingly in a daze, he entered the refreshment room where he had some beverages. About 2 p.m., he was found by one of the porters to be ill in one of the rest rooms. He seemed to be having difficulty breathing and so he was taken to the first class refreshment room and Dr Johnson of Spital Hill was sent for. Before the doctor arrived the young man was found to be dead and the time was recorded as being shortly before 6 p.m. A small sum of money was found in his pockets and a few letters indicating that he was a doctor's assistant, but it seems from the letter that he was not working at the time. He was respectably dressed in a black ribbed suit and a dark-coloured mackintosh. It is believed from the letters in his pocket that he came from Lincoln. The police ordered that relatives at the address be informed of his death.' (*Evening Star*)

DECEMBER 9TH

1852: On this day a discussion took place as to whether a female penitentiary could be established as the means for reclaiming 'degraded' females. The meeting, which was held in the Council Hall, received a deputation from the clergy and gentlemen of Leeds who already had a Lock Hospital (for women with syphilis) which had been in existence for over ten years. It was reported that: 'They had also established an asylum where they were able to reclaim some of these unhappy women who were so much enchained by the men who made a trade of them. It was impossible for these women to escape from such an existence and many had been reclaimed by being taken in by friends or received into service'. Revd J. Livesey said that there didn't appear to be such women in Sheffield, but the Revd R. Jackson disagreed, stating: 'In Leeds, for every known fallen woman, only two lived in houses of ill-repute'. Mr W.S. Brittain said that when he was a member of the Watch Committee he was astonished at the number of prostitutes recorded. It was agreed that a Provision Committee would be formed to look into it and thanks was given to the deputation from Leeds. (*Sheffield Free Press*)

DECEMBER 10TH

1844: Today it was announced that a room has been taken on George Street, over the workshop of Messrs Ellis and Hardwick, where persons desirous to purchase property to qualify themselves as freeholders would be welcome. In these rooms, in order to vote in the West Riding elections, people may obtain information as to property available which may be purchased at advantageous terms. The *Sheffield Iris* stated that: 'We particularly urge upon our friends their immediate attention to this matter. The purchases must be made before the 31st January to enable them to claim to be placed upon next year's registration. We trust the free traders of Sheffield will not be backward in this most important movement. It involves no pecuniary sacrifice, but will add immensely to the popular power. At the office we have mentioned, our friends may be informed of arrangements by which the property may be obtained with an extremely small cost in conveyance, and by which they may also be saved from all the vexation they have hitherto endured. These are advantages of great moment and will not be despised. It is anticipated that there will be many numbers of persons desirous of purchasing these properties and an early visit would therefore be advised'. (*Sheffield Iris*)

DECEMBER 11TH

1819: Today for the first time, the *Sheffield Independent and Commercial Register* was published by Henry Andrew Bacon from his premises at 9 Snig Hill, Sheffield. He assured his public that as proprietor that he 'has but two objects in view in my new publication, namely the security of British Independence and an amelioration of the present condition of the British People... conducted with true British Spirit. I dare to hope it will be supported by every Englishman.' He stated that the newspaper was set to contain a miscellany, so necessary for the general readers of newspapers, which would be carefully attended to and the latest intelligence up to the hour of publication would be given. Among the variety of other topics which would merit peculiar consideration, there was to be up to date information covering Commerce, Trade and Manufacture, as well as Agricultural issues. The advertisement noted that 'Mr Bacon trusts a distinguishing feature of his journal will be everything relating to the local interest and improvement of Sheffield and the neighbouring towns'. (*Sheffield Independent*)

DECEMBER 12TH

1940: This was the date of the first major evening air raid on Sheffield, which took place under the code name Operation Schmelztiegal (meaning Crucible) by the Germans. It was recorded that there had been a total of 406 aircraft allocated for the raid, which started at 6.15 p.m. and lasted until 4.17 a.m. the next morning. It was reported that at 8 p.m. some incendiaries had fallen around Norfolk Street, and Nether Edge Hospital was hit by three bombs. Five people were killed and a baby was born during this part of the raid. However, at 11.45 p.m. the Marples Hotel in the town centre was hit, and of the seventy-seven people sheltering in the basement, only seven were rescued alive. By 11 p.m. many water mains had been fractured, and water had to be pumped a considerable distance. Around 11.35 p.m. a large explosion led to the destruction of Neepsend Gas Works. It was reported that every building on Angel Street was either bombed or on fire and King Street was said to be an inferno.

A second raid took place on December 15th and after the war it was assessed that 693 people had been killed and a further ninety-two were missing. (Vickers, J.E., *The Unseen, the Unsightly and the Amusing in Sheffield*, Hallamshire Publications Ltd., 2nd revised edition, 1997)

DECEMBER 13TH

1856: Today's *Sheffield Free Press* carried a warning to local farmers to look after their pigs to prevent them from being stolen by thieves. The article read: 'LOOK AFTER YOUR CHRISTMAS PIGS – An incident occurred on Saturday night, which should set as a caution to many of our industrious artisans in the suburbs of the town, to look well after the safe keeping of their pigs, intended for Christmas cheer. During the night some thieves entered the premises of Mr John Gaunt, of Darnall House, and then slaughtered a fine, fat pig, which they carried off, leaving the entrails etc behind. There was no sound made during the robbery although the door to the shed which had been locked had been forced open. The pig was judged to be of 15 or 16 stone in weight. As pigs do not bear killing so quietly as most animals, it is supposed that the animal was first knocked on the head, or stupefied with chloroform. The police have requested that if anyone has any information about this robbery, they should be informed that Mr Gaunt has offered a reward of £25 for any information about any of the thieves that will lead to a conviction.' (*Sheffield Free Press*)

DECEMBER 14TH

1832: This day saw the Election Riots in Sheffield. At 10.15 p.m., a detachment of the 18th Irish Foot brigade, commanded by Captain Graves and attended by T.B. Bosville Esq., JP, were ordered to march up Waingate and form a line in front of the Tontine Inn. Stones were thrown at the soldiers and Mr Bosville was struck over the head with a stone. The military was ordered to fire and twenty men and a corporal fired ball cartridges upon the mob, and continued to fire as instructed by Hugh Parker Esq. JP and Henry Walker JP. Three men and two boys were shot dead, and several persons including two watchmen were shot and wounded. A very short space of time occurred between the arrival of the soldiers at the Tontine and the order to fire, which was estimated to be about five minutes.

Later evidence of T.B. Bosville was given to the coroner at the inquest on Jesse Fretwell, aged 19, who had died on the 31st after being wounded by the military on the 14th. The verdict given by the jury was 'justifiable homicide'. (Hey, D., *A History of Sheffield*, Carnegie Publishing Ltd, 1998)

DECEMBER 15TH

1839: The *Sheffield Independent* today reviewed a visiting circus owned by Mr Batty, whose performances were reported as being 'varied and interesting'. The reporter stated that: 'Monsieur Plege, the celebrated rope dancer, made his appearance on Monday and has nightly contributed to please and astonish the audiences, which we are sorry to say are only indifferent in number. This wonderful performer is very appropriately styled in the advertisements as by far the most elegant, graceful and surprising rope dancer we ever saw. Massotta too, the French equestrian, may be truly considered one of the cleverest riders of the day. In fact he appears to be fully equal to any task of horsemanship, and his performances have deservedly won the thundering shouts of applause of his gratified audience. Mrs Hughes also deserves great praise and we doubt much whether her equal can be found in the equestrian circle. Of the rest of the company it is only just to speak favourably, and to those who have not seen them, we heartily recommend them to lose no time in doing so'. An advertisement on another page stated that 'Mr Hughes the manager will take his benefit on Monday night under the patronage of the Master Cutler and other gentlemen'. (*Sheffield Independent*)

DECEMBER 16TH

1830: On this day it was reported that two Sheffield people had committed suicide in different parts of the town. 'Mr John Hague, land steward to Lord Wharncliffe, in a momentary fit of insanity, plunged the blade of a sword stick into his body and expired within a very few minutes. It appears that this unfortunate individual had for some time displayed such a disordered state of mind and that his friends had removed from within his reach every implement of self destruction, but the sword stick, which unfortunately they overlooked. An inquest has been held on his body and a verdict returned according to the circumstances related. On the same night at 6 p.m., Sarah Parkinson, a young married woman barely twenty-one years of age, threw herself into the river on Green Lane, although the reason for this act is not known. After the lapse of almost an hour, a shawl and bonnet which she had left near the water's brink, caused an alarm and the body was recovered, still exhibiting, it is said, some signs of life. The ordinary means of resuscitation were used by a passer by who was a medical man, Mr Clarke, but without any successful effect'. (*Sheffield Independent*)

DECEMBER 17TH

1835: Today it was announced in the *Sheffield Mercury* that at one of the late meetings of the Sheffield Public Baths Committee, that two gentlemen were deputed to visit several towns, in which public baths have been operating for some time, and report back to the committee. 'The result of their investigations has been most satisfactory. It appears that in the towns they have visited, the public have duly appreciated these valuable institutions. The receipts have much exceeded the smallest expectations of those interested in introducing such baths at Sheffield. So well satisfied are the committee with the information which has been obtained, that with one or two exceptions, they have all doubled the amount of shares which they had previously subscribed for. It was agreed that members of the committee will now look around for a suitable site on which the baths can be built. There have been several suggestions of sites and they will attempt to find the one nearest to the centre of the town.' The reporter announced that 'We are glad to embrace the present opportunity of informing our readers, that the committee of the Sheffield Water Company have made a most liberal offer of supplying the baths with water'. (*Sheffield Mercury*)

DECEMBER 18TH

1855: A young man of seventeen had a fatal fall on ice which resulted in his death. 'Beckett Dodson was the eldest son of Mr Edward Dodson of Handsworth Hall, who died suddenly during the previous night. On Saturday, he and his brothers were sliding upon a pond at Handsworth, when the deceased fell down on the ice and injured his head. Making little of his injuries, he and his two brothers subsequently went to Darnall station to meet two young friends, who came to spend Christmas with them. On reaching home the young man told his parents about the fall, but once again made little of the incident. Later he complained of a pain in his head and spent some time lying upon the sofa, although he refused to let his parents call a doctor and brushed off their concerns. He was induced to go to bed at an early hour and afterwards was joined by his two brothers, who preferred to sleep three-in-a-bed as a consequence of the cold. Next morning Beckett Dodson was found dead between his two brothers, having no doubt succumbed from the effects of the fall upon the ice.' (*Sheffield Independent*)

DECEMBER 19TH

1835: 'Three small boxes were delivered at Sheffield coach office today addressed to Messrs David Miller, Rose and Hobson, three dealers in different parts of the town. Mrs Miller was about to open the box when her husband came into the room. He was suspicious of the box and examined it more carefully. He found that one end had been put in last, fastened with screws and putty put over them to disguise them. He removed the box into an adjoining empty building, and having fixed a rope and a half hundred weight, he allowed the weight to fall on the box. Looking at the remains of the box he could see about six pounds of gunpowder, and water was instantly applied to saturate the box and prevent an explosion. Anyone opening the box such as his wife was about to do would ensure their instant death. Mr Miller applied to the coach office and ascertained that two other boxes had been delivered. He stopped one box from being delivered and the other from being opened. He had been told that they had been put on the stagecoach at Chesterfield. Suspicion has fallen upon a party to whom one of the boxes was directed and he has been taken into custody.' (*Sheffield Iris*)

December 20th

1860: It was recorded in a police report that on this day a robbery took place at an ivory warehouse in Burgess Street, to the value of £140. 'The warehouse owner, Mr John Banks, reported the robbery to the police, and a carter named William Smith was arrested. Within a few hours of his arrest, the whole of the contents of the robbery were recovered. Smith had confessed to the police that the stolen ivory had been placed in a cellar, which had been dug for the purpose beneath a garden house at Neepsend. The cellar was concealed from the view of passers-by and was in complete darkness, having no window to let in the light. On the first search, which was made without light, the property was not found, but on a lantern being obtained the stolen ivory was discovered on shelves placed all around the cellar. The cellar was so designed that it was ideal for concealing stolen property, and it is hoped that its discovery will frustrate the plans of the thief or thieves, who have been using it for some time past. Smith will be taken before the magistrates tomorrow morning and charged with the theft'. (*Sheffield Independent*)

DECEMBER 21ST

1846: Today, the weather was reported as being a little less severe than other years yet there was still a heavy frost during the night. 'Once or twice throughout the day there have been slight falls of snow, but even the hills and adjacent moorland are not thickly covered, as might be expected at this time of year. Nevertheless many of the dams are frosted over, which has delighted some of the young people who have held skating competitions on them. Yesterday a young man caught his skate on a stone embedded in the ice on Little London dam and landed on his head so hard that he broke the ice. Thankfully some of his friends were on hand and he was pulled out of the icy water. He is now recovering at home. Some inconvenience has already been experienced for want of water to drive the mill works on the River Sheaf and for several mornings the streets have been glazed over with ice and there has been a few accidents from people slipping on the ice. Last night rain started to fall about 8 p.m. which turned to snow about midnight, but thankfully had disappeared by the morning of December 21st.' (*Sheffield Times*)

DECEMBER 22ND

1827: Preparations for the Christmas festivities were in full swing and three pies were sent off to London from Sheffield. 'Three pies have been made by Mr Robinson, the late cook of the Tontine Inn, from Mr Walker confectioner. The three together weighed upwards of fifteen stone and they took over eight hours to bake. They are called ornamental raised pies and cost over fifteen guineas each. The pies are remarkably well baked and contain; three geese, three turkeys, four hares, fifteen pheasant, four grouse, ten partridges, four tongues, four woodcocks, four fowl and one leg of veal, one leg of mutton, 10lbs of ham, 14lbs of pork, four rabbits, four snipes, six pigeons, 6 stone of flour, 14lbs butter, 10lb of suet and twenty eggs. Exhibited at Mr Turners was one of the largest pies seen for miles around which will be eaten on Christmas Eve. It measured the following size: one yard and a half long, two feet wide, one foot deep and ten feet round. It was baked by Mr Barlow and judged to be "quite perfect" the crust consisting of six stones of rye meal. The pie will be shared amongst the poor people of the town.' (*Sheffield Courant*)

DECEMBER 23RD

1855: This evening the town of Sheffield was delighted to play host to Charles Dickens, who was reading his tale *A Christmas Carol* in the Mechanics Institute. The *Sheffield Independent* stated: 'He was an expert at injecting into these well known characters, so distinctive a life, and to every sentiment, an appropriate tone. Expressions of approbation, peals of laughter and rounds of applause were given in happy spontaneity, followed Mr Dickens from beginning to end. At the close of the reading the audience cheered so enthusiastically, that all present seem to have acquired a sudden increased power of hands and voice. The ex Mayor, Mr William Fisher, ascended the platform to thank Mr Dickens, which led to renewed cheering in tumultuous delight. The Mayor, Mr W. Fawcett, then presented the author with a very handsome service of cutlery and stated that "he hoped that he would have a long life and live to wear them out". He told him that although he had read *A Christmas Carol* before, he would always now associated it with this evening and the Christmas of 1855. Mr Dickens replied with such warmth and assured him "the gift will long remain an heirloom in his family as a reminder of the towns warmth and generosity of the hearts of the people of Sheffield".' (*Sheffield Independent*)

DECEMBER 24TH

1843: Today's newspapers held an account of the trial of three Sheffield prisoners, John Smith, Charles Dawson and Harriet Johnson, who had been found with twelve pieces of false coins in Sheffield on November 29th last. 'On that day the police had arrested Dawson in a garret at his lodging house, whilst in the very act of coining base money. More money was found on him, which had just come from the mould and was still warm. The other prisoners were in the room and they had on their persons some base metal, a quantity of plaster of Paris and two iron spoons. Two days earlier Dawson had taken the room and had asked the landlady for a fire in his room, but she had refused, saying that the bed was too near the fire, and she had no coal. On the forenoon of the day in question, she had gone out and had locked the door leading to the garret. When she returned she found the door had been forced, and so determined to have a fire that the prisoners had used part of the bed head to making one. She called the constable and they were found with the base coins on them. All were sentenced to ten years' transportation.' (*Sheffield Iris*)

DECEMBER 25TH

1871: 'A traditional Christmas Day was celebrated at Sheffield workhouse today, when the guardians once more provided the inmates with a dinner of roast beef and plum pudding. The dining hall had been beautifully decorated by the inmates, with evergreens and artificial flowers, and shortly before noon upwards of 400 of the inmates came marching in and dinner was served. Some idea of what was eaten may be gathered from the fact that the dinner consisted of 70 stones of prime beef and 85 stones of pudding. Several of the guardians, the master and the matron and some of the medical officers were present, as well as a number of visitors. Alderman Hallam (chair of the board of guardians), Mr Searle, Mr Muddiman and Mr Widdison delivered brief and appropriate addresses after the dinner and the health of the officers of the workhouse was drunk. The previous master of the workhouse, Mr Westoe, was likewise present and his health was drunk very vociferously. Thanks were given to the guardians by the master. In the afternoon the men were plentifully supplied with tobacco, the women with snuff and the children with oranges.' (*Evening Star*)

DECEMBER 26TH

1900: Today was the second performance of 'Babes in the Wood' at the Theatre Royal in Sheffield. The *Sheffield Guardian* wrote: 'Seldom if ever has a first night performance passed with greater smoothness into what must eventually prove an assured success, than that presented on Christmas Eve at the Theatre Royal by the excellent Company, which has been got together to interpret the Babes in the Wood. People are always prepared to make the greatest allowances when a new play is produced for the first time; but the artists at the Royal needed very little encouragement. From the leading boy down to the humblest player there was a clockwork-like precision throughout the entire performance. Mr F. Leslie Morton was responsible for the book and the pantomime is being produced by him under the direction of Messrs H.H. Morrell and Frederick Mouillot. The story of the Babes runs through twelve scenes and the artists are to be highly complimented on the loveliness of the pastoral and realistic groupings of the architectural scenery'. (*Sheffield Guardian*)

DECEMBER 27TH

1851: It was reported today that a man had died of apoplexy whilst playing cards. Michael Annesley, an Irish labourer, had been playing cards with another one of his countrymen when he keeled over. He had a winning hand and he was chuckling with success and thrown his cards down on the table when he collapsed. His son sent for a surgeon but by the time he arrived fifteen minutes later, the man had died. During the inquest the jury was told that Mr James Gregory, the surgeon, had been sent for but he refused to attend. The jury considered his behaviour to be reprehensible and sent a request that he attend the inquest and account for the refusal. The gentleman explained that he had so frequently been called upon to attend drunken quarrels in Coalpit Lane, for which he was generally insulted and rarely paid, that he did not feel called upon to go out on such occasions. On that night he was expecting to be called out on a difficult case of labour. The explanation was satisfactory to most of the jury, although there were others who considered that even though a surgeon may be called on sometimes unnecessarily, it was his duty to go. (*Sheffield Free Press*)

December 28th

1882: Today's *Sheffield Post* announced the arrival of a new Act of Parliament which was to affect all the women in England. 'As the clock strikes out the last hour of this rapidly dying old year, there will come into operation a modest Act of Parliament, which gives to married women the absolute control of their money and other property. This will be a bad job indeed for the money hunters and, like Othello, they will find their occupations gone. It is stated that many widows are waiting till the beginning of the New Year before allowing themselves "once more to be enchained in the locks forged by Hymen". This of course may have been a stretch of the imagination; but it was suggestive of the caution widows are prone to observe. Henceforth ladies will have but themselves to blame if they are married for their money. The Act will prove a blessing to many a married woman, whose ill-fortune it is to be married to a man who acts on the principle of what's hers is mine and what's mine is my own. Henceforth her savings and her wages become her own property.' (*Sheffield Post*)

DECEMBER 29TH

1869: On this day was printed an account of a snowball riot which took place on the Corn Exchange on Sunday afternoon. 'About four o'clock during a snow storm about 200 "roughs", mainly made up of men and lads, gathered together and took shelter in the Corn Exchange building. Soon they began to amuse themselves by throwing snowballs at persons who were passing by. One such man, Mr William Ashton, was struck in the eye by such a missile containing a stone, and smarting with pain, he turned back to revenge himself. It was unfortunate for him that he did so, for his assailants at once joined in an attack on him, and knocked him to the ground. Several of the men began kicking him in a very brutal manner. By this time police constables Bestwick and Unwin arrived, and the gang rushed off in all directions. They apprehended one of the ringleaders, Samuel Woodhead, who was described as "a lad" and who was brought into the magistrate's court this morning. The chief constable stated that the prisoner had already been locked up for two nights following the snowball riot and the Bench thinking this was sufficient punishment, discharged him on payments of the court costs.' (*Sheffield Times*)

December 30th

1899: 'A man was brought into the magistrate's court this morning charged with being drunk on Glossop Road. It appears that he was a respectably dressed man who gave his name as G.S. Ludlum and that he was a grocer and tea dealer at Broomhill. From the evidence of police constable Berry, it appeared that about midnight last evening he met the prisoner, drunk and in female attire. He had on a black silk dress, a shawl and a lady's muff and the constable, thinking that he had a very masculine appearance, took him into custody. The prisoner said that he had been to a party and had put the dress on "for a lark". His defence, Mr Dyson, stated that he had donned the female garb for a game of charades when drunk and had walked down the street without changing his clothes. The magistrate reported that there had been many cases before him of men living on the outskirts of town, frequenting the suburbs dressed as women and he stated "that kind of thing must be put a stop to". The bench fined him 40s and costs and he left the dock loudly protesting that he had done nothing to deserve such a fine'. (*Sheffield Star*)

DECEMBER 31ST

1827: The *Sheffield Courant* on this day describes an account from an officer passing through the town with his family who stayed at the Tontine Inn. He told a reporter that he had been stationed at Sheffield at the Tontine, with his regiment, at the time when Col Althorpe made his notable charge on the unfortunate multitudes in Norfolk Street (*see* August 6th 1795). He said: 'At the first intimation of a riot the officers were just dressing for dinner. I hastily donned my regimental and went into the mess room, which is the same room we are sitting in now. Having changed I took out of my pocket half a guinea and laid it on the chimney piece, but in a hurry to snatch it up I pushed it down the crevice of the chimney piece and could not recover it. Now if the chimney piece has not been removed the piece of gold is still there'. The newspaper goes on to say that: 'It is worthy of remark that last week the same chimney piece was taken down and the identical half guinea found. Should this account reach the officer it may afford him some pleasure to know that which was lost is now found'. (*Sheffield Courant*)

Visit our website and discover thousands of other
History Press books.

www.thehistorypress.co.uk